WHAT PEOPLE ARE SAYING ABOUT
TRUST ISSUES

Trust Issues will make you laugh, think, and pray. With gut-level honesty and grace-filled truth, Justin Graham invites you to confront the places where trust has been broken—by others, by yourself, and even in your relationship with God. If you're ready to heal from the inside out, this book is for you.

—Eric Petree, Pastor
Citygate Church, Cincinnati, Ohio

Pastor Justin Graham's book, *Trust Issues*, is a manual for believers on how to move through issues we encounter in everyday life that cause us not to trust. In the book, he is open, honest, transparent, and raw. He doesn't simply communicate well; he examples well. He doesn't just *tell* you how to lay aside the things that weigh you down; he *shows* you how to do it. His transparency draws us to a place of honesty and provides a blueprint for dealing with the deep issues life places in front of us. This book is a must-read for anyone who has been betrayed, hurt, misused, or abused and is ready to live beyond it and experience the freedom and fullness of life in Christ.

—Germain Brunson, Pastor
Louisville, Kentucky

As an avid reader, I have to say this book, *Trust Issues*, is one of the most well-balanced books I've read in a long time! Justin Graham's use of scripture and interweaving it into everyday real-time life is absolutely the best! Leaving you intrigued, laughing, and wiping tears from your eyes from beginning to end, it's a game changer. He will challenge the strength of your relationship with Jesus, encourage your involvement in your local church, and, at times, be so raw with his in-your-face coaching ability you will not want to put the book down. Any trust issues you may have hidden in your life will be peeled back like the onion of your spiritual, marital, practical, and kingdom life and revealed when you didn't think anyone could. This book is a must for believers and unbelievers of all ages. Justin writes with a passion for his readers to mature in Christ! You will think you're sitting with him, just chatting at the park or relaxing on the lake. Don't hesitate to read it and pass it along for others to enjoy.

—Tim Teague, Retired Pastor
Simplead, President, Morristown, Tennessee

A powerful and thought-provoking read from start to finish, *Trust Issues* by Justin Graham broaches important subject matter with rare vulnerability that compels the reader to go on a deep introspective dive into the interpersonal world of relationships where trust is at the core. If you are looking to improve your relational capacity, *Trust Issues* is a must-read.

—Ronnie Harrison, Lead Pastor
The Kingdom Center, Louisville, Kentucky

Timeliness is an understatement for this incredible word. Our world is filled with distrust, and it is fomented by the news media, social media platforms, and, sometimes, wolves in sheep's clothing! Beyond the intentional charlatans and liars, there are those who, through personal weakness and character flaws, disappoint us and trigger our distrust of others. Our knowledge of personal failures and weaknesses causes us to sometimes distrust ourselves. Stephen Covey, in his book on trust, made it crystal clear that when trust is high, the cost is low, and achievements happen quickly. On the downside, when trust is low, the cost is high, and achievements are painfully slow. This is not an informational book; it is a transformational book. Here's what I know: My pastor told me it takes a good man (vessel) to deliver a good word, and Justin Graham is on fire for God. Being around him is stimulating and encouraging. As you read this book, listen to the heart of the man—truthful, transparent, and in pursuit of a calling that is higher than even he realizes.

—Maury Davis, Pastor and Director,
Apex Ministry Network
Nashville, Tennessee

As I sit down to write this endorsement for *Trust Issues* by Justin Graham, I cannot help but reflect on the remarkable journey I've had the privilege of witnessing in this man. From his early days in college, navigating the complexities of faith and life, to his role as a devoted husband, father, son, son-in-law, dedicated youth pastor, assistant pastor, and, now, the lead pastor of one of the most vibrant churches I know, Justin's journey has been nothing short of inspiring.

The words within these pages delve deep into the vital importance of trust—trusting God amidst life's unpredictability and the call each of us has to be trustworthy stewards of His grace. Justin articulates the challenges we face in developing and maintaining trust, ensuring that readers understand the transformative power that comes from leaning on God in every circumstance.

I wholeheartedly endorse this book to every individual looking to grow in their faith and become a catalyst for trust in their communities. The insights Justin shares will encourage and challenge you, compelling you to experience all that God has for you—if only you trust Him. Enjoy the journey!

—Ron Martin, COG Administrative Bishop
Columbus, Ohio

Watching my husband write *Trust Issues* has been a beautiful journey—one marked by deep prayer, reflection, and an unshakable desire to help others walk in step with God. This book isn't just words on a page; it's a reflection of his heart, his faith, and his own wrestling with what it means to truly trust God—and to live in a way that God can trust him too. I've seen the way this message has transformed his life, and I know it will do the same for yours. If you're ready for honest, powerful truth that will draw you closer to God, you've found it right here.

With all my love and admiration,

—Melissa Graham, His Wife and Biggest Supporter
The Avenue Church, Morristown, Tennessee

Trust Issues is more than a book—it's a divine assignment. With wisdom, authenticity, and purposeful clarity, Justin Graham speaks as a chosen and trusted voice in the Kingdom, delivering a timely message that pierces the heart and strengthens the spirit. This isn't just about trusting God; it's about understanding what it means for God to trust you. A must-read for anyone ready to walk in deeper partnership with Heaven. He has been called and anointed to release this timely word. This book carries the weight of revelation and the invitation to genuine intimacy with the Father.

—Kevin Wallace, Pastor,
Redemption To The Nations Church,
Chattanooga, Tennessee

TRUST ISSUES

JUSTIN GRAHAM

TRUST ISSUES

ANSWERING THE **ONE QUESTION** THAT **CHANGES EVERYTHING**

AVAIL

Dedication

To the love of my life, and my very best friend, Melissa. I am forever grateful that God would allow me to be your husband. Every day with you gets better and better. I would not be the man I am today without your love and support. You are the most beautiful person in the world, and I love you with my whole heart.

To my gorgeous daughter, Jocelyn. You are the first one to call me "Dad." You've had my heart from day one, and you always will. Watching you discover God's call on your life is such an incredible joy. Turn the world upside down. You are an anointed woman of God, and I am so proud of you. "ILYMTAYS!"

To my handsome son, Judah. When I look at you, it's like looking into the mirror. You are determined, disciplined, and becoming an incredible Godly leader. I have always asked a lot from you because I believe in you. You are going to change the world. You are a man of God and will do greater things than I. "ILYMTAYS!"

To Jocelyn and Judah. Always remember something . . . if I have it, it's yours.

To my parents, Royce and Linda. When I was young, you held my hand, and as I grew, you helped me discover my wings. Thank you for being good stewards and raising me to know God. Today, I treasure the House of God because you taught me how to honor it. I hope I have made you both proud. I love you forever.

CONTENTS

ACKNOWLEDGMENTS

THANK YOU TO the best staff a Pastor could ever pray and ask for! Avenue staff . . . I love you more than you will ever know! Thank you for always having my back. Thank you for helping me carry the vision God has given us to make Jesus famous throughout the world. We've only just begun!

Thank you to my Avenue Church family. After being Melissa's husband, and Jocy and Judah's dad . . . it is the greatest joy to be your Pastor! Everywhere I get the opportunity to minister, I have the privilege of sharing how amazing you are. Thank you for being a Church that carries the heart of God and loves people like you do. Together, let's keep emptying hell and populating Heaven! I am so proud of you!

Avenue Board of Directors, Elders, and Pastoral Leadership Team—Thank you for giving me your shoulders to stand on. I love you BIG TIME! Adam Noe, Jason Williams, Todd Adkins, and Joey Rush—thank you for being my brothers. I would get in trouble with you and for you.

Dr. Sam Chand—Thank you for believing in me. Your love and priceless investment in me have forever changed my life.

Megan Adelson—Thank you for the countless hours you spent critiquing and coaching me in writing *Trust Issues*. You're a rockstar.

Avail Publishing Team—Thank you for your investment in this project. It has truly been an honor to work with you.

FOREWORD

EVERYONE TRUSTS . . .
You trust the electrical wiring you've never seen and the
electrician you don't know.

- You trust people at a traffic light that they will stop on red.
- You trust your pilot.
- You trust that you'll be paid.
- You trust your doctor's prescription.

Why is it easier to trust people we don't know than those we do?

Everyone trusts . . . till trust is broken!

Trust is the one thing that can build or destroy every
human relationship.

Trust is essential to high-level performance—everything rises
and falls on trust. People come to church because they trust. They
put their kids in kids' church / nursery because they trust. People
give financially because they trust.

Trust is daily between people and organizations at all
levels—it's daily.

Poor behavior by so many leaders in all sectors of life has created a general culture of mistrust.

Trust is built, not by big things but by small things such as
returning phone calls, responding to emails, being on time,

following through on commitments, paying back loans, and keeping confidences.

Trust is built incrementally. As assignments are fulfilled, more trust is deposited in the trust bank account.

Trust is the currency that can be used to buy and sell. . . . Trust can also be dissolved. Broken trust brings sanctions with it.

It takes a lifetime to build trust and thirty seconds to destroy it.

Broken promises—talk is not cheap. Making promises is buying something on a credit card—you don't have to pay right then, but you will pay. Deferring payment will cost you more in interest. Nonpayment will bring punitive repercussions and ruin your "credit."

Leaders whose behaviors do not match their message—"walk" vs. "talk." "Trust me," "Believe me," but many leaders are "Non-believable."

New team members might bring their mistrust from their previous contexts. If their behaviors in their new environment are the same as their previous place of service, they create "layers of mistrust," and they quickly become jaded and cynical like the rest. Lack of trust begets more lack of trust.

It is harder to regain trust on the character level than on the competence level.

"It's not that I cannot forgive you—it's that I cannot trust you!"

Regaining trust is the most difficult thing a human being can do at any level of relationship.

People can trust the persons and not the process or trust the process and not the people.

Trust is a psychological contract requiring reciprocity.

Trust is developed slowly but lost quickly and is difficult to regain.

Just because you love someone doesn't mean you trust them with everything. When my kids were young, I loved them, but I did not give them the car keys or let them cook ... trust grew till one day that happened.

Trust is a feeling based on repeated reality.

We create feelings of trust but only if our repeated reality and experience are close to expectations.

My friend Pastor Justin Graham will lead you to discover your trust issues.

We all have them!

Sam Chand
Leadership Consultant and author of *Leadership Pain*

INTRODUCTION

I **WILL NEVER FORGET** the day my man card was temporarily suspended. The very first time (and only time) I ever drove a motorcycle, I wrecked and almost broke my wife's leg.

I was ashamed to even look her in the eyes!

Cozumel, Mexico, was one stop on our first cruise together. There, we could rent motorcycles (not scooters) to drive around and explore at our leisure. My wife thought it would put us in a romantic chick flick movie setting, while my overprotective and cautious self could only think of how this would put us in some kind of horror film. She batted her eyes, and I took a deep breath and gave in to her request.

It was an overcast and misty day, but still extremely beautiful. As we rented the bike, the gentlemen warned us to use extreme caution—the cobblestone roads get dangerously slick when wet. At that, I immediately regretted my decision not to stand my ground. I tried to play it cool, but my anxiety was through the roof! Thoughts of death, broken parts, and fireballs stormed my mind! I did my best to hide my fear and look like a professional bike rider. Before I had time to consult with my wife, we agreed to everything they told us, and off we went to enjoy our romantic day in Mexico. After a few minutes of battling through the stress, anxiety, and probably high blood pressure, I started gaining confidence to navigate a motorcycle as a rookie. Nothing could have gone better as we enjoyed what felt like paradise.

It was time to head back to the ship and return the bike to the rental company, but the only way to get there was to make a U-turn because there was no cut-through in the median. As I turned on the cobblestone and gave it a little gas, the bike started to fishtail, and we slammed into a parked car on the side of the road! The engine burned Melissa's leg, pinning it between the motorcycle and the parked car. My fear had come true! Our romantic excursion had turned into a horror movie! I thought, *Great, I'm a loser; my wife is going to divorce me, and I'm going to jail in Mexico!* Thankfully, the owner of the vehicle I hit was so kind, as was the owner of the motorcycle. They allowed us to pay a little extra to take care of the minor damages. My wife's leg was not broken; it was just burned pretty badly but would eventually heal. So, in case you're wondering, Melissa didn't leave me, and I didn't get arrested. However, the loser question is up for debate.

One thing is sure: On that romantic day in Mexico, I gave my wife *TRUST ISSUES!*

TRUST

Merriam-Webster defines trust as "assured reliance on the character, ability, strength, or truth of someone or something. One in which confidence is placed."[1] Trust can and will make or break you.

---

1   *Merriam-Webster Dictionary*, s.v. "trust," accessed April 8, 2025, https://www.merriam-webster.com/dictionary/trust.

> ## WHEN TRUST IS EARNED, A REAL TREASURE IS DISCOVERED. AND WHEN TRUST IS COMPROMISED, A HEART IS BROKEN.

It can be a source of great strength, or it can be a source of great frustration.

It can lead to great friendships, or it can tear apart life-long relationships.

Trust affects families, marriages, friendships, churches, communities, businesses, and even entire nations!

It is not only a gift that you give; it is a gift someone gains. When trust is earned, a real treasure is discovered. And when trust is compromised, a heart is broken.

Trust is very complex. In the Bible, God instructs, encourages, and even commands us to place our trust in Him. In Proverbs 3:5, He tells us to trust Him with our whole heart. He can do that because, one, He's God, and two, His track record is flawless. He has never given us a reason to have *trust issues* with Him, but when someone does us wrong, we blame Him and suddenly develop *trust issues*. Sometimes, it may feel like we cannot trust God when we hit life's dark seasons and rough patches.

Again, trust is very complex and can produce many questions. Does our ability or inability to trust God directly affect our trust in others? Is our lack of trust in God the root of our trust issues? Trust issues can cause us to feel stuck, and our reasons for struggling with trust can be endless. Honestly, it's really easy to point the finger at God and/or other people because it takes the heat off of you. Could it be that the cause of your trust issues is centered around YOUR actions? *Maybe you don't trust God because, in reality, you cannot be trusted.* As difficult as it may be to come to that conclusion, no one knows you better than you know yourself, and sometimes, it's easier to deflect fault onto God or someone else.

So, the heart of this book will deal with hard truths and help you answer some questions:

- Can I trust God?
- Can God trust me?
- Am I trustworthy?
- Have I caused others to have trust issues?
- What must I do to gain or repair trust?

> **MY HEART IS BROKEN BECAUSE I'M WATCHING PEOPLE TURN AWAY FROM GOD BECAUSE OF TRUST ISSUES.**

It is believed that Warren Buffett said, "Trust is like the air we breathe. When it's present, nobody really notices; when it's absent, everybody notices." The consequences of broken trust can be detrimental! In this book, you'll discover that your compromises cause others to have *trust issues!* Many of us don't want to believe that we could be compromising when, in reality, we're the problem.

My heart is broken because I'm watching people turn away from God because of *trust issues.*

Generations are leaving the church because of trust issues!

Christians have left churches because of negligent, reckless, and untrustworthy pastors!

Marriages are failing because of unfaithfulness, which has broken trust!

Leaders have lost influence because of trust issues!

Fathers have lost respect because of their lack of integrity!

Mothers have lost their hearts because of compromise!

Friendships have been severed because of trust issues!

Businesses have lost customers because of trust issues!

America is divided because we don't know whom or what we can trust!

In the age of AI and endless social media platforms, we are flooded with half-truths, lies, and false realities!

And now, more than ever, we are seeing celebrities in the entertainment industry hide behind hidden agendas that suck us in and suck us dry as we believe everything we see and hear!

We've watched those we've looked up to, admired, and trusted fall flat on their faces, and now, we don't know who or what can be trusted!

WE HAVE TRUST ISSUES!

You might be saying, "Amen!" but pointing out and celebrating everyone else's flaws and mistakes is not the goal of this book. This book is an invitation to dive deeper into your issues. Do you trust **GOD**? Can you trust **GOD**? Can God trust **YOU**? Are **YOU** trustworthy? Have **YOU** broken trust? Have **YOU** compromised and given others trust issues? The good news is that all is not lost. While my wife may never get back on a motorcycle with me, I have worked hard to prove that she can trust me with the things that matter most—and continue to do so.

As you read this book, my heart is for you to ask yourself the hard questions and pray as David prayed in Psalm 139:23-24, "Search me, God, and know my heart; test me and know my anxious thoughts. See if there is any offensive way in me, and lead me in the way everlasting."

You might be thinking, *I'm a trustworthy person, so if my trust-worthiness is tied to my trust in God, shouldn't I trust Him more than I do?* I pray this book will help you change your perspective about the two-way street of trust. At the end of each chapter, take the time to meditate on the "Big Ideas," answer the questions, and pause long enough to pray the written prayers. Let's commit now to diligently gaining God's trust and the trust of anyone and everyone we have the opportunity to influence!

Could it be that God's greatest blessings, breakthroughs, and miracles are simply waiting for you to heal the *trust issues* between you and Him? Let's deal with our *trust issues*... today!

PART ONE

IN GOD
WE TRUST

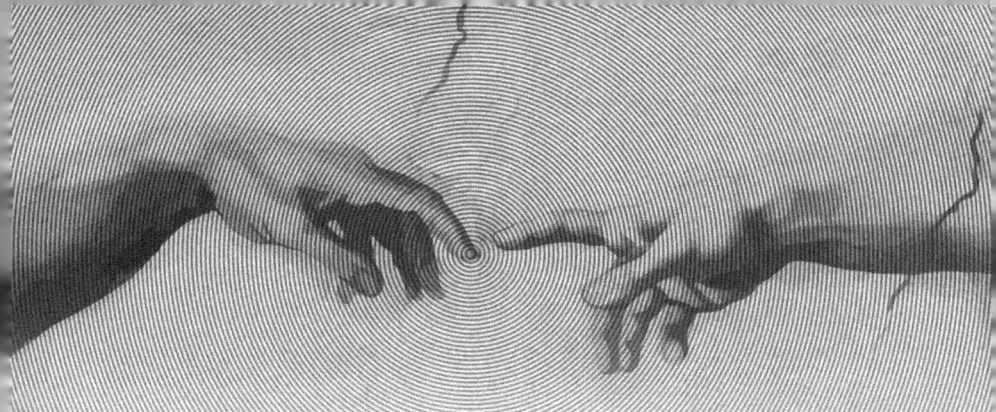

CHAPTER 1

CAN I TRUST YOU?

I'**LL START FROM** the beginning. One day, I knew—beyond a shadow of a doubt—that God had spoken to me. That day has forever marked me and changed everything about me!

My wife and I decided to take a massive leap of faith when we launched The Avenue Church in January 2013. What started with nine people has turned into a movement—almost ten thousand decisions to follow Jesus! (That's a story for a different book, though.)

Very early on in this journey, I was driving home from my office on what I thought was just a very normal day. I took a left turn onto a street I had driven thousands of times and, at this point, my thoughts were on autopilot. *I can't believe God has let me pastor a church! I think things are going well. I wonder how my kid's day was at school? Should I try calling Melissa again . . . because she just loves to ignore my calls? Are there any games on tonight? What are we going to do about dinner?* As I passed Apostle Road, there was a voice like thunder that shook my soul and pierced my heart! *CAN I TRUST YOU?!* My heart felt like it was about to pound out of my chest because I knew that voice was not my own. That moment changed everything for me!

Without any hesitation, I knew I was experiencing the Lord's omnipresence as He sat down in the passenger seat of my truck to ask me the most important question of my life.

CAN I TRUST YOU?! I heard again. And then a third time, *CAN I TRUST YOU?!*

It's hard to explain, but it's as though a million thoughts flashed through my mind in a split second. I thought, *This is it! God is about to reveal something He's never shared with anyone else on the face of the earth!* That thought was immediately followed by, *Wait, why did He have to ask me, though? Why couldn't He have just told me that He trusted me?* So, my zealous, innocently over-confident self replied, *Absolutely, God, You can trust me!* I have to be honest; initially, I felt pretty awesome. I was fired up because I knew I had just heard from the Lord! The entire moment felt like an out-of-body experience. Little did I know that He was not even close to being finished with me.

I continued my drive home; my heart was racing, and I was eagerly waiting and hoping for a different response from Him. It would have been amazing if God had said, "Justin, you're a rockstar, and I'm so impressed with you. And because you're the most trustworthy person in the world, I'm about to let you in on a secret." Instead, all I kept getting over and over again was, *CAN I TRUST YOU?!* Eventually, I could no longer tell if He was asking me again and again or if the question was just ringing in my spirit.

I pulled into my driveway, and I heard, *CAN I TRUST YOU?!*

I greeted my family, and all I could hear was, *CAN I TRUST YOU?!*We sat down to eat; I watched bits and pieces of a ball-game, helped the kids with homework, helped with the dogs, helped get the kids to bed, and all I could hear on repeat was, *CAN I TRUST YOU?!*At that point, I was confused. I finally lay down in my bed and put on an episode of *Everybody Loves Raymond*,[2] like I do almost every night because I'm the ultimate processor, and shows like that sometimes help me turn my mind off. It helped me escape my thoughts, and I tried to drift off to sleep. However, there was no sleeping that night.

Don't get me wrong, I was, and still am, extremely grateful that God took the time to speak to me that night, but I became so grieved and worried because I realized that my previous answer was not what He was looking for at all. I began to question so many things about my life. Was God disappointed in something I had done? Was He upset with me, and this was His way of correcting and disciplining me? My confident "yes!" was turning into a very uncertain, "I hope so, but I don't know."

I got up earlier than usual that following morning because, after not sleeping all night, I didn't need an alarm clock. Melissa and I went about our morning routine of getting the kids up, taking care of breakfast, and getting them ready for school. After dropping them off, I was alone in my truck, or so I thought. All the way to the office, all I could hear was, *CAN I TRUST YOU?!*I pulled up to the church and gathered for prayer with the staff like we do every morning, but then, I went to the altar and completely crumbled in the presence of the Lord. I cried out to God, *Why do*

2   *Everybody Loves Raymond*, Philip Rosenthal (New York, NY: September 13, 1996, CBS), Television.

you keep asking me this question? At first, it was so easy to answer, but now I don't know. Maybe You can't? Am I doing something wrong? What do I need to do? It was there, in that place of brokenness, that He began to share what He really needed me to fully comprehend. It wasn't just a question. What He shared with me next has never left me and never will!

Like a sponge soaking up water, I began to listen and hang on to every word. *Justin, I need to be able to trust you. If I can't trust you, I won't do what I really desire to do in your life. If I can't trust you, it will limit your whole life, including your family and the church. I must know that with everything I do, you will never make it about yourself, but you will give me all the credit and make it all about Jesus. And I have to know that, with every blessing, you will never compromise your integrity.* **Can I trust you?**

I wiped my tears, picked myself off the floor, took a deep breath, and finally understood why God had kept asking me the same question.

TRUST: THE FOUNDATION OF ALL RELATIONSHIPS

All relationships hinge on trust because it determines how productive and successful they will be. Trust is nonnegotiable if you're going to build a life that honors God and gain confidence and respect from others.

In the Bible, we discover the most incredible story of trust. If you haven't read Genesis through Leviticus, I really encourage you to do so because a lot happened. In Genesis, God creates the whole world and all of mankind. He placed them in a garden, allowed them to enjoy the beauty of His creation, and gave them only one rule. It was only a matter of time before man went behind His back and did the very thing they were instructed not to do.

Trust issues!

Over time, God became angry with mankind because trust had been completely destroyed. He wiped out the entire human race with a flood, saving only Noah and his family. He used Noah to start fresh, so to speak, because everyone else had become evil, and no one could be trusted. After the flood, God established His covenant with Abraham, his son Isaac, and his grandson Jacob (also known as Israel). This family was blessed and became the people of God. In Exodus, the Egyptians enslaved God's people. However, God's hand was on them, and He had a plan to set them free. By the time you get to the Book of Numbers, God has assigned a man by the name of Moses to be the deliverer for His people, the Israelites, who have been in slavery for hundreds of years. Long story short, Moses led the Israelites on a journey to the land that God had promised them. Everything seemed to be going great until it wasn't.

Moses's assignment was a huge undertaking because he would have to lead somewhere around a million people through the desert without Google Maps or Siri. So, God supplied him with help and support from his own brother and sister, Aaron and Miriam. As time passed, the Israelites began to complain about the hard conditions of the desert, but Moses didn't have access to a Sam Chand or a John Maxwell to learn good leadership. Instead, Moses did the best he could to obey God and instruct everyone on how to handle living arrangements. Then, things started to get out of hand. The people were getting mad at Moses, God was getting angry at the people for complaining, and to make matters worse, Moses's own brother and sister turned on him! Talk about *trust issues*! The two people he should have been able to trust the most had complained about him behind his back.

God caught wind of this and was not happy, so He called all three of them together. Check out God's word to them in Numbers 12:6-8 (NLT):

> *"If there were prophets among you, I, the LORD, would reveal myself in visions. I would speak to them in dreams. But not with my servant Moses. Of all my house, he is the one I trust. I speak to him face to face, clearly, and not in riddles! He sees the LORD as he is. So why were you not afraid to criticize my servant Moses?"*

What a mess! We'll talk about that more in chapter 3. What I want to bring to your attention is what the Lord said to them in verse 7: *"Of all my house, he is the one I trust."* Now, that's a statement! God was saying that, out of the millions of His people, Moses was the one He trusted.

Trust.

The word *trust* used here is the Hebrew word *āman*. It means "prove to be firm, reliable, faithful, permanent; to believe in; to be firm, secure; to accept as true."[3] In other words, Moses had proven himself trustworthy. He was the one God believed in. The one God could rely on. The one God had faith in. God didn't have any *trust issues* with him. Moses was the one God trusted!

---

3   Douglas Mangum, Derek R. Brown, Rach Klippenstein, and Rebekah Hurst, *Lexham Theological Wordbook* (Bellingham, WA: Lexham Press, 2014); Mark E. Biddle, Ernst Jenni, and Claus Westermann, *Theological Lexicon of the Old Testament* (Peabody, MA: Hendrickson, 2004).

Can you imagine the God of all creation saying that about you? "Of all my house, _____ is the one I trust."

Do you feel confident enough in your track record to write your name in that space?

FILL IN THE BLANK

Early on in ministry, I had the opportunity to keep building trust with my wife or completely shatter it. I had just laid down for the night, and I did what a lot of us do today—I pulled out my phone and checked my texts, emails, the news, and social media. I noticed I had a new message in my Facebook Messenger, so I checked it out. It was someone from the church who had sent me a video message from either her couch or her bed. She addressed the video to me and my wife but only sent it to me. Let's just say it was very strange. Immediately, I remembered the question, *CAN I TRUST YOU?*

> **WHEN IT COMES TO TRUST, THE LITTLE THINGS MATTER JUST AS MUCH AS THE BIG ONES . . . IF NOT MORE!**

Melissa was downstairs, so I called out to her and told her to come see the video for herself. Needless to say, she was not happy! For a moment, she put her "pastor's wife" card away and was ready to take out her earrings and make a visit! We handled the situation pastorally—with truth, love, and grace—to make sure that the lady understood the appropriate boundary lines. To this day, I don't look at or respond to any social media messages. What if I had replied to her? What if I had not told my wife about the video? Talk about *trust issues!*

"*Of all my house, _____ is the one I trust.*"

Or how about this one? Joel Osteen, the pastor of Lakewood Church, once told a story of trust that, to some, might not seem like a big deal. He was in a hurry, on his way to meetings, taking care of some errands, and had to make a stop at a store. After he parked his car, he opened the door in a rush, and the wind swept through and blew a napkin and papers across the parking lot. The parking lot was mostly empty, and he thought, *Nobody will see that. I can just let it go.* God spoke to him immediately and said, *That's not integrity, and that's not trustworthy.* So, even though no one would see him, Pastor Osteen walked across the parking lot to collect what had flown out of his car.

> **IT'S ONLY WHEN WE FINALLY DECIDE TO GET HONEST THAT WE'RE ABLE TO MAKE THE NECESSARY CHANGES IN OUR LIVES.**

When it comes to trust, the little things matter just as much as the big ones ... if not more!

"Of all my house, _____ is the one I trust."

Can you be trusted to always do the right thing?

Can your family trust you? Can you be trusted with that business deal?

Can you be trusted to lead your church with integrity?

Can your spouse trust you to be faithful in thought and action?

Can you be trusted to handle the finances?

Can you be trusted when someone pours their heart out to you?

CAN YOU BE THE ONE THAT GOD TRUSTS?

With all of my heart, I want to joyfully shout to God, "YES! You can trust me!" But that scares me to death because I know myself better than anyone else. I don't like what I'm about to say, but unfortunately, it's true. *I haven't always been trustworthy, and I have caused many trust issues throughout my life.* That statement makes me want to puke and really messes with my mind and emotions. But it's only when we finally decide to get honest that we're able to make the necessary changes in our lives. And the hard truth is, I'm still working on that every single day. We'll dive more into this concept later on.

> **TRUST IS NEVER JUST GIVEN.
> TRUST IS ALWAYS EARNED!**

Moses did not have God's complete trust and confidence because he woke up one day and decided to be Israel's deliverer.

Moses was in his eighties when God broke the news to him, and just in case you didn't know, when you get to that age, you've seen some stuff!

God watched Moses for eighty-plus years and realized there was something special about him. There were plenty of ups and downs, highs and lows, mountains and valleys, blessings and challenges, but through it all, God liked what He saw and gave Moses His approval. What an incredible honor!

News flash: You are not a trustworthy person just because you say you are! Can I take us back to a well-known fact that we should have learned at a very young age? Trust is never just given. Trust is always earned! Moses worked hard to gain God's trust. Without a doubt, there were some long nights and hard seasons. There were some good decisions and even some bad ones. There were some accomplishments and some disappointments. And to ease your mind that you are not disqualified, Moses messed up throughout his life. He made some really bad mistakes! In fact, I've devoted a whole chapter of this book to that! Yet, in the long run, God liked what He saw and placed His hand of approval on Moses.

"CAN I TRUST YOU?!"

The day the Lord asked me that question has forever changed my life! God was not asking me for a *verbal reply*; He was asking for a *lifestyle response*! He was asking for my faithfulness. He was asking for my loyalty. He was asking me to live a life that would eliminate His *trust issues* with me. God was calling me higher to be someone He could trust, and as you're reading this book, I'm asking you the same question.

> **WHILE YOU MAY NOT BE ABLE TO FIX EVERYONE ELSE, YOU SURE CAN WORK ON THE ONE IN THE MIRROR.**

Can God trust you? Because He wants to do some really awesome things in your life! *Can others trust you?* Because this world is deficient in faithful and reliable people! We've witnessed one too many moral tragedies in marriages, politics, entertainment, businesses, and pulpits. It's time to eliminate *trust issues* in your life. While you may not be able to fix everyone else, you sure can work on the one in the mirror. Take the time to seriously examine your heart and allow God to work in you; surrendering to this process will produce a greater trust in God that will flow out of you more naturally. He will help you make the necessary changes in your life, and other people will notice.

> *"Many a person proclaims his own loyalty, but who can find a trustworthy person?"*
> —Proverbs 20:6 (NASB)

Your spouse needs someone they can trust!
Your boss needs someone they can trust!
Your church needs someone they can trust!
Your friends need someone they can trust!
Your teammates need someone they can trust!
Your followers need someone they can trust!

JUSTIN GRAHAM

God is looking for people He can trust!

WORK ON THE HINGE

All good and thriving relationships hang on the hinge of trust. In other words, the door opens and closes. Traffic flows in and out. And I believe that your trustworthiness affects how much you trust in God. Whether or not you can truly trust God depends on how honest you are when you answer the question, "Can I trust You?" You can and should trust God, but maybe you're struggling to see His trustworthiness. One reason why you struggle to trust God may be because you don't trust yourself. You know all of your failures, so you question whether you could ever truly be trusted. If you don't trust yourself, how can you ever fully trust in God?

> ## HONESTY IS THE SOLUTION
> ## TO REAL LIFE-CHANGE.

My home office sits between my bedroom and my son's room and directly across from my daughter's room. The door to my office squeaks at the same angle when I open and shut it, enough to be pretty annoying, especially when I'm up late studying while my wife and kids are sound asleep in their rooms. No matter how quiet I try to be, I risk waking someone up when I open and shut that door late at night. When I open the door, it squeaks, and when I shut it, it squeaks. The squeaking won't stop unless I fix the hinge. I risk waking others up from their rest if I don't fix the door. Likewise, your failure to deal with your trust issues will directly impact others in your life! Your heart is the hinge that needs your attention. Trust is a heart issue. If you want to give and earn trust, then start being more intentional about working on your heart.

Can you be trusted?

I'm not asking for a verbal reply; I'm challenging you to evaluate your heart and life. Will you get honest with yourself and get honest with God? Honesty is the solution to real life-change. It's so much easier to trust God when you address and deal with the trust issues in your personal life. Will you rise to the occasion? I believe in you! As we continue on this journey, we're going to align ourselves with God's Word and do whatever it takes to be the one God and others can trust. I pray you will work hard to eliminate trust issues in your life.

HERE'S THE BIG IDEA:

Actions speak louder than words. If you want to gain someone's trust, save all the good lip service—prove it by living with godly integrity!

CONSIDER:

- In what areas of your life have you compromised and caused trust issues?
- What are some things you can do to help reestablish trust?
- How has your own lack of trustworthiness affected your ability to fully trust in God?

CHALLENGE:

- Humble yourself before God and ask for His forgiveness for your sins and any disobedience.
- If necessary, humble yourself before the person you've hurt and/or broken trust with and ask for their forgiveness.
- Discipline yourself to make the right decisions based on God's Word, regardless of the circumstance.

PRAYER:

Heavenly Father,
Will You please forgive me for the things I've done that
have compromised Your and others' trust in me? I desire to
reflect Your love and faithfulness through the way I live.
Will You please help me do the hard things, the right way,
no matter what it costs me? In Jesus's name. Amen!

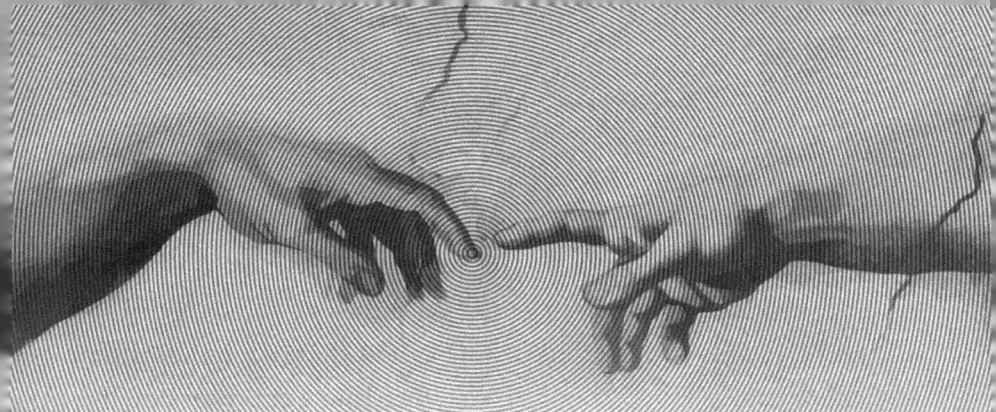

CHAPTER 2

'TIS SO SWEET

OUR GREATEST EXAMPLE of trustworthiness is God! Life is a blessing, but it will throw you some curve balls and send you through the ringer to give you trust issues. Through it all, I'm realizing more and more that God is faithful. He has proved Himself, time and time again, that He is trustworthy through the ups and downs, the highs and lows, the blessings and battles, and the mountains and valleys.

I'm a church junky. I grew up in church. I come from the old school tradition (which is the good school) of being in church every time the doors were open. I was at choir practice every Sunday morning. After practice, I went to Sunday school. After that, I went to children's church, or "big church," depending on my age at the time. Once church let out, we would grab lunch, hang out for a while, maybe hit a Sunday nap or parts of a ballgame, and then head back to choir practice to prepare for our evening service. That was my Sunday every week. As the week went on, we returned to church on Wednesday night for service. Not one time throughout my childhood and teenage years did my parents ever ask me if I wanted to go to church! At times, I told them I didn't feel like going, to which they always replied, "That's okay; we didn't ask you." So, off to church we went!

I was born and raised at the Morristown Church of God, and a couple of hundred people called that place their home church as well. I was born in a hospital, but I'm pretty sure they put me in the church nursery the next day. When I was a young kid, our worship team consisted of a piano player and sometimes an organist. We had what some called a "cattle call" choir. I remember before our Sunday evening services, someone would ask if anyone else wanted to join the choir with the rest of us. People would come up and sing whether or not they could hold a note. Now, that's what I call *trust* because some of them sounded like actual cattle!

> ## YOU DON'T REALLY TRUST SOMEONE UNTIL YOU'VE WITNESSED THEM COME THROUGH ON THEIR WORD.

Service after service, we would sing songs that I'm pretty sure were around when Moses was leading the Israelites. I liked some of them, but some of them were questionable. A song that always stuck out to me was "'Tis So Sweet to Trust in Jesus," by Louisa M. R. Stead. The precious people of our church would get so excited and passionate as they sang these lyrics:

'Tis so sweet to trust in Jesus, Just to take Him at His Word;

Just to rest upon His promise;
Just to know, "Thus saith the Lord."
Jesus, Jesus, how I trust Him,
How I've proved Him o'er and o'er,
Jesus, Jesus, precious Jesus!
O for grace to trust Him more.[4]

At the time, I didn't realize the profound truth behind this song; I just thought, *Man, they really like this song!* Little did I know that this song would take on a whole new meaning later in my life.

After high school, I ended up in Cleveland, Tennessee, where I attended and graduated from Lee University. I was a part of Lee's Campus Choir where I met my best friend and beautiful wife, Melissa. We got married and graduated in 2003 and then became youth pastors in January of 2004 in Cincinnati, Ohio, at the Central Parkway Church of God. We were green as grass, pumped about life, floating on cloud nine, and could easily sing and shout, "'Tis so sweet to trust in Jesus!" But at the time, never once did I think about whether He could trust me.

You don't really trust someone until you've witnessed them come through on their word.

Before God ever let anyone know that He trusted Moses, He spent time showing Moses what it meant to be trustworthy. Understand this: *When God makes a promise, He keeps it!* God showed up and introduced Himself to Moses on the back side of the wilderness. He spoke to Moses through a burning bush and told him to go to Egypt to bring the Israelites out of slavery.

4   Louisa M. R. Stead, "'Tis So Sweet to Trust in Jesus," by Louisa M.R. Stead, hymn, public domain.

God promised Moses that He would be with him through it all and lead them to a land where they would become a great nation and people. In that moment, God performed a couple of miracles to prove to Moses that He could be trusted. Moses agreed and headed off towards Egypt, where he would witness God perform ten miracles that would ultimately lead Pharaoh to set the people free. Remember, when God makes a promise, He keeps it!

When Moses led over a million people out of Egypt, Pharaoh had a change of heart and chased them all the way to the Red Sea to trap them. But God came through on His word by splitting the waters, allowing the Israelites to cross over on dry land. God then used those same waters to crash over the Egyptians who were trying to kill them. God was proving that He could be *trusted!*

When the Israelites journeyed through the desert, God led them with a cloud by day and fire by night. *He was proving that He could be trusted!* When they had nothing to drink, God drew water out of the rocks. *He was proving that He could be trusted!* When they had nothing to eat, God provided food every morning. *He was proving that He could be trusted! Again, you don't really trust someone until you've witnessed them come through on their word.*

THE TRUST FALL EXPERIMENT

There's an old game or trick that I'm sure you have tried a time or two in your life. It's called a "Trust Fall." It works like this: Your friend stands behind you to catch you as you fall backward—a true test of how much you trust them. The real test comes as you totally release control without turning around or looking and completely fall into their arms, allowing them to catch you just before you hit the ground. You're either amazed that they caught you just before you hurt yourself, or your friend is disappointed because you resisted the fall and didn't trust that they would catch you. This is the perfect example of trust issues. I wonder how God feels when we allow ourselves to fully fall into His arms so that He can work out every challenging situation in our lives. And I wonder how He feels when we stop short of trusting Him and take matters into our own hands. Psalm 37:5 (NLT) says, "Commit everything you do to the LORD. Trust him, and he will help you." I can't encourage you enough to *trust fall* into the arms of God *because when He makes a promise, He keeps it!*

Three years into youth pastoring in Cincinnati, Melissa and I had our first child, Jocelyn. The following year, we had our second, Judah. While those were two of the greatest days of our lives, they still required putting two kids in diapers at one time. For those of you who are parents, you know how expensive it is to raise kids. We thought we had a good grip on life while balancing family and ministry until things started falling apart. I woke up one morning and headed downstairs to get some laundry out of the dryer. As my feet left the bottom step, I landed in several inches of water. Our entire basement was completely flooded! We had to hire a company to install a sump pump system around the foundation of our house. It cost us $13,000, which we didn't have in savings. The following week, our vehicle decided to stop working. That cost us another $2,000. In a matter of a couple of weeks, we were $15,000 in debt!

Melissa called me at the office that next week in tears, worried we wouldn't have enough money to cover the essentials we needed that week, like diapers and formula. Without any hesitation, I told her, "We're going to be fine, but no matter what, make sure you write our tithe check to the church." Her anxiety and stress rose a little more because she couldn't get the numbers to work. I remember hanging up the phone, and as I rested my head on the back of my seat, I could hear that "cattle call" choir from my childhood singing, "'Tis So Sweet to Trust in Jesus." I believe God's Word about tithing, and His promise in Psalm 37:25 (NIV) says, "I was young and now I am old, yet I have never seen the righteous forsaken or their children begging bread."

A couple of days passed, and someone called, saying he and another guy had something for me and wanted to meet at the church with the pastor. In the pastor's office, they shared how God had put it on their hearts to bless me and Melissa with a financial gift. They wrote us a check for $15,000! In a miraculous moment, God showed me that He could be trusted! *'Tis so sweet to trust in Jesus!*

A couple of years later, I drove from Cincinnati to Knoxville, Tennessee, to meet my dad and watch our Auburn Tigers beat the Tennessee Volunteers on their field. It was a great night! After the game, I said my goodbyes and started the drive back to Cincinnati so I wouldn't miss church the next day. It was a night game, so by this time, it was really late. As I got to Lexington, my wife called me on the phone and was hysterical. Judah had a croup cough because of a viral infection, and he was really congested. He hadn't been sleeping well and was up late coughing really badly. Melissa got him out of bed to help him, and in her arms, our son stopped breathing and was turning blue. She was screaming and crying on the phone, and I told her to call 911 and start praying. I hung up the phone and called out to Jesus to touch my son and breathe life back into his body. I turned my flashers on and floored it to get to my family as soon as possible. I was crying, praying, and *trusting*!

A few moments passed, and my wife called me back. She was crying but not hysterical. Her tone had changed entirely as she began to tell me, through tears, that while she was on the phone with 911 and praying, God suddenly breathed life into Judah's body. He took a deep breath and started to cry! The ambulance showed up and took my son to the hospital in Cincinnati, where I pulled in right behind them. That should tell you how fast I was driving! I never recommend that, but I was desperate to get to our son. While at the hospital, the doctors told us that Judah would be completely fine, and nothing was wrong. God had healed our son! In another miraculous moment, God showed me that He could be *trusted*. *'Tis so sweet to trust in Jesus!*

Melissa and I *trusted* God to leave what was really good in Cincinnati and follow His call to launch The Avenue Church in Morristown in 2013. In case you're wondering, church planting is not for the faint of heart, but everything was going well for the most part. A couple of years into it, we were faced with a good problem. We were growing as a church and had to decide what to do with our facility space. There were three options on the table:

Option #1: Buy half of the facility.

Option #2: Buy the entire property.

Option #3: Expand but continue to rent until we could afford to purchase.

We met with our elders and collectively agreed to fast, pray, and trust God for direction. I met Melissa at a Zaxby's restaurant on the last day of the fast. We were simply talking about life when I paused and poured my heart out about the building situation. I told her I wasn't certain what God wanted, but thinking about option #3 allowed me to breathe. I raised my hands and said, "I know any renovations and remodeling would cost us a few hundred thousand dollars. I just wish God would give me $100,000 to confirm my feeling."

The very next day—less than twenty-four hours later—my phone rang while I was out on the field coaching flag football. I answered. It was someone who lived out of state but had been following what God was doing at The Avenue Church. I knew this person from attending the Morristown Church of God together when I was younger. He and his wife were in town for a couple of hours and asked if they could meet us at the church. He said they would love to see all that God was doing at our facility. I told him to give me about an hour. We walked them around the church for a few minutes and shared some of the amazing things God had been doing in so many lives.

As we were about to head out, he said, "Before we leave, we want to be obedient to what God told us to do for you." He then proceeded to hand me a folded-up check. Now, you don't just open up a check in front of the person who gave it to you. So, I put it in my pocket and thanked them for their love and support. He smiled and said, "I know you're trying to be polite, but we want you to open it." I opened it, started to cry, and almost fell out in the Spirit. It was a check for the church for $100,000! My wife saw it, and she started shouting. They were obviously curious about our reaction. Through my tears and shock, I told him about the building, the fast, and the proposition I had given God less than twenty-four hours before that moment. They were in shock, too, but it gets better! He told me that the check had been written for months; he was just waiting for the right time to give it to us. Now, we all were crying and celebrating the faithfulness of God! In another miraculous moment, God showed me that He could be *trusted. 'Tis so sweet to trust in Jesus!*

> **SOMETIMES, GOD WILL ALLOW UNCERTAINTY TO PROVE HIS FAITHFULNESS AND TRUSTWORTHINESS TO YOU.**

Allow me to testify with one more story because I want to build your faith in the goodness of God. Fast-forward a couple of years and our church was ready to purchase the entire property to continue to build and expand to reach more people for Jesus. Through lots of prayer, fasting, and *trusting*, we decided to purchase our current piece of property and buildings for 4.2 million dollars. Now, to muddy the waters, one acre of the parking lot was not a part of the property. However, we were told and understood that it would not be an issue to acquire that additional acre once we purchased the property. So, we signed and celebrated.

The very week we signed the papers, we were informed that that acre of land had actually been sold to another company, but no one knew who owned the property. Everywhere we turned led to a dead-end. We finally found out that Taco Bell had purchased it and planned to build a restaurant that year on that acre. I would love to tell you that I didn't panic, but I can't. The thought of having a Taco Bell in the middle of our parking lot terrified me. I remember asking God, *Really? We just purchased this land, and now this? Did we make the wrong decision?* I was not thinking about how sweet it is to trust in Jesus. I was freaking out!

> ## WHEN GOD MAKES A PROMISE, HE ALWAYS TAKES CARE OF EVERYONE INVOLVED.

I finally collected myself, and we started praying, fasting, and *trusting* God. What we thought was a *setback* was actually a *setup*. Sometimes, God will allow uncertainty to prove His faithfulness and trustworthiness to you. A gentleman from Taco Bell reached out to a precious lady in our church and asked if she would like to manage one of their new restaurants coming to our area. The address she saw confused her because it was the church's address. We connected with them to explain our situation after she told us about their conversation. The gentleman I spoke with is a good Christian, and the situation devastated him. They were under the impression that we were moving, and he assured us that he would have never purchased the acre of land in the parking lot if they had known we were staying. It was a mess! At that moment, I had to remind myself of Proverbs 3:5-6 (NIV), "Trust in the Lord with all your heart and lean not on your own understanding; in all your ways submit to him, and he will make your paths straight." I chose to *trust* God's Word.

The gentleman was so gracious and received approval to look for another location. If they could find another location, they would let us purchase that acre back from them. Long story short, a precious family who owned the corner lot across the street at the main intersection was willing to work with Taco Bell to sell them their land, which was the land that Taco Bell wanted to begin with. So, we were able to purchase that acre of land in the middle of our parking lot, where we would eventually build our new sanctuary! He not only showed His trustworthiness to me and Melissa but also to Taco Bell and the landowners! When God makes a promise, He always takes care of everyone involved.

Those months were filled with stress and anxiety, but they reminded me of how sweet it is to trust in Jesus! Oh, and I had never liked Taco Bell, but now, I go there and support them . . . gladly! In fact, every day, I drive by what I now call The Miracle Bell, which sits right across from our church!

I could go on and on with story after story of how I have witnessed the faithfulness of God. I *trust* Him because I have proved Him "o'er and o'er," as the song states. *When it comes to trust, God has a perfect track record!* You can *trust* Him when the answer to your prayer is "yes," and you can *trust* Him when the answer is "no." No matter what you face, you can rest assured that He will work all things for your good.

I'm so thankful for my parents, who kept me in church where I learned about *trusting* God! In so many of life's challenges, I can still hear that choir singing, "'Tis So Sweet to Trust in Jesus!" I learned that if God did it for them, then He would do it for me, and I'm telling you—it really is so sweet to *trust* in Jesus! He is faithful! *You can trust God! If He did it for me, He can and will do it for you!*

If God can part the Red Sea for Moses . . . He can make a way for you too!

If God can provide food and water for millions of people in the desert . . . He can provide for you too!

If God can pay off our flood damage and car repair debt . . . He can open heaven over your life too!

If God can breathe life back into our son's lifeless body . . . He can bring healing to your life too!

If God can provide me with $100,000 for the church . . . He can show up right on time for you too!

If God can provide Taco Bell with the right land . . . He can work out that scary situation for you too!

I wish I could tell you that I've never struggled to trust God. Sometimes, I've had to convince and remind myself of just how much I could trust Him. *This thing called life is a* **trust fall.** It may feel like you're about to hit the ground, but God will be there to catch you! He just needs you to *trust* Him!

> **I BELIEVE YOU NEED TO DO EVERYTHING YOU CAN IN THE NATURAL AND ALLOW GOD TO DO WHAT ONLY HE CAN IN THE SUPERNATURAL.**

'TIS SO SWEET TO TRUST IN JESUS!

Could the reason nothing's changing be that you haven't fallen into God's arms? Maybe you're too busy taking matters into your own hands. Maybe you're stressing yourself to death trying to fix the situation. I'm not saying you should sit on your hands and do nothing. I believe you need to do everything you can in the natural and allow God to do what only He can in the supernatural. Do your part! Keep praying, keep believing, keep fasting, and keep *trusting*! Learn to rest in the fact that God "is able to do immeasurably more than all [you] ask or imagine" (Ephesians 3:20, NIV, author addition). Maybe you're unrestful because you think you can fix the situation when actually, *you're not resting because you're not trusting!* You have *trust issues because when you work, God rests, but when you rest, God works!* When you try to fix what only He can handle, you tie His hands. He has to rest. But when you decide to lean back and *trust* that He is more than able to work things out for you, He works!

— JUSTIN GRAHAM

I never learned to trust God on the mountaintops where everything is great! I learned to trust God when He allowed me to spend time in the valley!

News flash:

You'll never trust Him as your Healer . . . until you've experienced sickness!

You'll never trust Him as your Provider . . . until you've had to do without!

You'll never trust Him as your peace . . . until you've stared anxiety in the face!

You'll never trust Him as your joy . . . until you've lain awake at night with depression!

You'll never trust Him to give you victory . . . until you've had to face some battles!

You might be saying, "I hear you, Justin, but you just don't understand what I'm up against." And you're absolutely right. I don't. But I do know the One who is more than able to make right everything in your life that you think is wrong! He can handle your fear, your stress, your anxiety, your anger, your doubt, and even all your *trust issues*. In fact, we'll tackle that more in the next chapter. As you read this book, I pray you discover how sweet it is to trust in Jesus!

He leads by good example. So, in turn, I challenge you to follow Him and become trustworthy. Together, we're going to deal with all our *trust issues*!

HERE'S THE BIG IDEA:

Trusting God is so much easier said than done, but it is so worth it. If you learn to lean on Him, He will always care for you and work all things for your good!

CONSIDER:

- Do you struggle to trust God? If so, why?
- Does letting something go and allowing God to have full control of your life scare you?
- If so, why?
- In what areas of your life do you need to practice trust falling into God's arms?

CHALLENGE:

- Reflect on your life and recall all the ways God has come through for you.
- Write those moments down in this book or a journal, and let them build your faith and trust in Him!

PRAYER:

Heavenly Father,
Thank You for all the times You have proven Yourself trustworthy.
Thank You for every blessing and time You have protected and provided for me. Please forgive me for not recognizing that it was You the whole time. Help me to lean back in Your arms and trust that You will take care of my life and work all things for my good. It really is so sweet to trust You! In Jesus's name. Amen!

JUSTIN GRAHAM

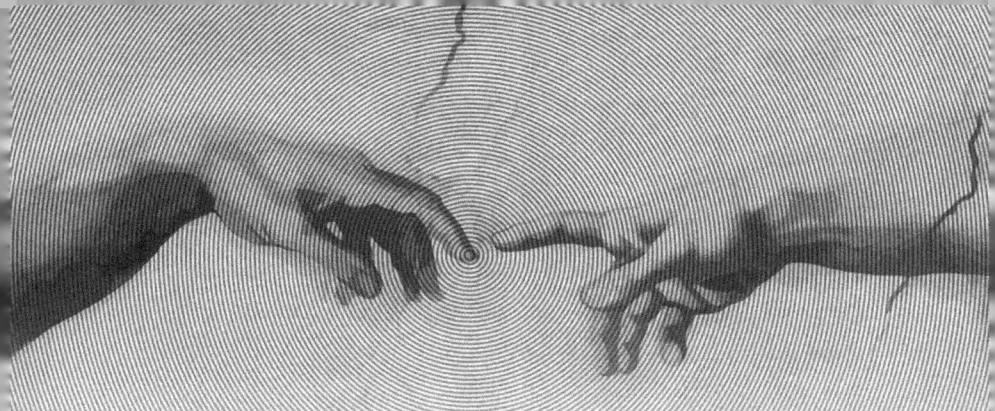

CHAPTER 3

I DON'T TRUST GOD

LOUISA STEAD WAS born in England in 1850. At a very young age, she developed a passion to, one day, be a missionary. When she turned twenty-one, she migrated to America and lived in Cincinnati, Ohio. There, she attended a church service where her desire to become a missionary grew stronger, but her health complicated those plans. She eventually got married and had a beautiful daughter named Lily. Life had been good to them, and everything was great!

Around 1880, on what seemed to be a typical day, Louisa and her husband took their daughter, Lily, on a picnic on Long Island Sound. While they were enjoying the day, cries for help reached their ears from a young boy who was struggling to swim and about to drown. So, Lily's dad took off in hopes of rescuing him. Unfortunately, his attempt failed, and both Lily's dad and the boy drowned.

In one moment, life went from great to tragic, from so much joy to unbearable grief. Louisa headed out that day with what some would call a picture-perfect family, only to come home as a broken and shattered single mother. Their world was torn apart as Lily watched her own father—her hero—fight the waters to save his life and that of the little boy. They both had to stand there, helpless and hopeless, when he went under the water for the last time and never resurfaced.

As they tried to pick up the broken pieces of life, Louisa and her daughter were left to struggle financially without the income that he provided for their family. They were desperate. *What do you do when your faith and trust in God only lead to pain and heartache?* In the darkest season of her life, filled with hopelessness, pain, sorrow, uncertainty, and grief, she didn't turn away from God; she turned *to* Him! It was in the middle of this crisis that she picked up her pen and wrote:

> *I'm so glad I learned to trust Him,*
> *Precious Jesus, Savior, Friend.*
> *And I know that He is with me,*
> *Will be with me to the end.*
> *Jesus, Jesus, how I trust Him,*
> *How I've proved Him o'er and o'er.*
> *Jesus, Jesus, precious Jesus,*
> *Oh, for grace to trust Him more.*

Trusting in God looks good on paper—it's so easy to say but can be extremely challenging to do, especially when life throws you unexpected curve balls. So, I understand that your faith might not look like Louisa's . . . yet. She seems like a faith rockstar! Take the pressure off of yourself because your faith doesn't have to be as big as Louisa's for God to prove Himself faithful. The Bible tells us that God needs just a little bit of faith. If you are in Christ, God has promised you faithfulness. He will meet you where you are. However, it can be irritating when someone tells you to just trust God. You might be thinking, *I tried trusting Him, and look where it got me. I don't trust God! Where was He when my spouse was unfaithful to me? Where was He when I lost my job? Where was He when I lost my loved one? Where was He when the person I trusted betrayed me? Where was He when everything I believed to be true was actually a lie?* Do you want to go there? Let's go!

On a Monday morning in early 2012, I was on my knees in our church sanctuary in Ohio, working with some audio cables because we'd had sound issues that had disrupted the previous day's service. I was a youth pastor, but when duty called, I was also a sound engineer. It was on that stage, working on some cabling issues with no one around, that I knew I had to step out in faith and do what I felt God was calling me to do. For almost an entire year, I had been wrestling with what He had been stirring in my heart. I will never forget this moment because it nearly took my breath away. My heart was racing, and I was starting to feel clammy as I stood to my feet and headed to my pastor's office. I knocked on his door, he welcomed me in, and I asked if I could talk with him. I took a deep breath and started to weep. I finally spoke the words that I had tried to suppress for the past year, "I think I'm supposed to pastor a church in Tennessee!"

I was so nervous to even talk about it. There were so many thoughts running through my head: *I haven't even talked to my wife yet. Everything is great where we are now. You can just stay here and pastor this church one day. What if I'm wrong about this, and we're not supposed to go to Tennessee?* My pastor sat back in his chair to process what I had just dropped in his lap. I'm very thankful for this man who was so gracious to me. As much as he wanted me to stay there, he wanted more than anything for God's perfect plan to unfold in our lives. To this day, he is our biggest fan. I left the office that day feeling like I had lost my mind and went home to my wife to share with her what I had been trying to avoid for a year.

When I spilled the beans, she smiled and said, "I have felt the same thing but was waiting on your lead!"

I'm a crier, so I started crying again! That day, we decided to trust that God would help us work it all out.

Melissa completed a job application in Morristown to test the waters. Immediately, she got offered the job, and now I was really freaking out! We made several phone calls and connected with some people we trusted about where we felt God was calling us in Tennessee. We were greeted with much excitement and, many times, were encouraged to make the move. After several of those calls and an in-person meeting with them, we were convinced the move was right. So, we decided to take a massive step of faith, leave everything, head to Tennessee, and completely trust God! It was the scariest thing we have ever done. God only gave us one step—move to Tennessee. So, until we received our next instruction from Him, I would be unemployed, carrying both the burden and desire every man has to provide for his family. It was a complete trust fall into the hands of God! There were so many unknowns. What would this look like? Would we plant a church? Was there a church that needed our help? All we knew was that we were in it to win it! We trusted God and were ready to help reach people for Christ.

WHERE GOD LEADS, HE WILL ALWAYS PROVIDE.

The people we connected with several months earlier invited me to a meeting a couple of weeks after we arrived in Tennessee. I was told we would discuss the next steps after the meeting. We were fired up! I was anxious and excited at the same time. As the meeting approached, I could hardly wait to discuss the plans with those who had encouraged us to make the move. After the meeting, I raced up to the front to greet one of those people, only to hear, "Oh, yes, Justin, I don't know what you want from me; I can't help you." At first, I thought it was a joke. And then, I quickly realized he was actually serious. As I stood there, I had to make a decision that would impact the future of not only my family but also the future of our ministry. Would I continue to trust God?

I could have gotten angry with them because they lied to me. I didn't. I could have tucked my tail, cried a river to God, and complained about how it wasn't fair. I didn't. I could have stormed off, jumped in my car, and yelled at God about how all of this was His fault. I didn't. I could've chosen to get bitter at God and discouraged enough to quit the ministry. I didn't. Instead, I looked back at them and said, "Oh, well, thank you anyway." As I walked off to my car, I decided to trust God no matter what happened next because where God leads, He will always provide. One man's "no" is God's "yes." Sometimes, God has to close the wrong door so you can see the right door He's already opened. In the middle of stressful uncertainty, God gave me supernatural peace. Despite the bad news I had just received, God immediately revealed our next step to me. I called my wife and shouted, "Are you ready? Because I now know what we're supposed to do!" The rest is history. We trusted God and launched The Avenue Church the following January of 2013, and since then, we've witnessed God do the impossible over and over again! We have seen almost ten thousand people decide to follow Jesus because we trusted that God knew what He was doing the whole time!

If you're struggling to trust God—whether it's with something in your life or because of something that's happened to you—I get it. It's so easy to point the finger at God when something hurtful or unfair happens. Besides, if He's in control, He allowed it to happen, right? However, could it be that God *allowed* it so that He could work *in* it to fulfill His purpose for you? I encourage you to continually remind yourself that the season you're in is not the whole story. You're just in the middle of one chapter.

TRUSTING GOD SEEMS COMPLICATED

It was during the most difficult time of Moses's life that God made it known to the Israelites—and now to us—that Moses was the one He trusted. He was tasked to lead millions of people through the desert to a Promised Land with no prior experience. He'd never led an entire nation. He'd never been a CEO. He'd never been a pastor. He'd never started a business. He simply had to do his best to lead, trusting God through it all. The Israelites witnessed God perform numerous miracles through Moses's leadership that helped them place their trust in him. However, it seemed like things were starting to spiral out of control. People started complaining about their hardships in the desert, and in return, God became angry with them. His promise to bless them with freedom and their own land was met with grumbling and complaining. So, the Lord set parts of their camp on fire! Moses stepped in and called out to God for mercy, and the fire died out.

> **TRUSTING GOD WILL NOT ALWAYS MAKE SENSE, BUT IT WILL ALWAYS BE WHAT'S BEST!**

Then, the Israelites started complaining about the food. They ate the same thing day in and day out. I love Zaxby's chicken and Mexican food, but I wonder how I would feel about it after eating it for breakfast, lunch, and dinner for days, weeks, or months in a row! So, they said they wished they could go back to being slaves in Egypt. At that point, Moses was done! In fact, he told God that the weight of his responsibility to lead the people was too great, and if He wasn't going to help, then he would rather die. To top things off, Aaron and Miriam turned on Moses, stirring up trouble and talking against him. Remember, Aaron was Moses's brother, and Miriam was their sister. The two people whom he should have been able to trust the most betrayed him!

If anyone knows about trust issues, it's Moses! He's the one who experienced all the chaos! He's the one who endured the constant rebellion and backstabbing! He's the one who suffered betrayal from his own family! If anyone should have had trust issues, it was Moses.

How could Moses keep trusting in the One who appointed Aaron, who had turned on him, to be his right-hand man? Was Aaron and Miriam's betrayal God's fault? Did God cause it? Yet, through it all, Moses continued to place his trust in God. It was through the pain that God positioned him for greatness. It was in the face of adversity that God elevated Moses to a place of honor and authority. One reason God trusted Moses was because of how he dealt with the betrayal—he kept trusting God even when others were careless with their actions.

Trusting God will not always make sense, but it will always be what's best!

What do you do when your faith in God and your trust in Him leads you to pain and heartache?

How do you trust Him again when the people God provided betray you?

How do you trust Him again when your spouse, whom God gave you, decides to have an affair?

How do you trust Him again when a member of the family that God chose for you sexually abuses you?

How do you trust Him again when everything that was supposed to be of God and from God falls apart?

How do you trust Him again when the godly leaders in your life lie to you?

What do you do when your faith in God, and your trust in Him, leads you to sorrow, brokenness, and disappointment?

How do you trust Him again when a pastor or church leader—meant to represent Him—falls morally and is exposed as living a lie?

We live in a world full of people who have trust issues because of the careless actions of others!

PEOPLE ARE NOT GOD

I've been in full-time ministry for over twenty years and in church from the time I was born. I love church! I believe in the local church! However, I am so sick and tired of scrolling through the news and learning of another church's or pastor's scandal or moral failure! My heart breaks every time and is quickly followed by anger as I wonder how someone could be so careless and stupid. I was eight years old when the news hit about Jimmy Swaggart's moral failure. At the time, I didn't fully grasp the magnitude of the stain it left on the church. I remember thinking I would probably never hear about something like that again. Then, as I became a minister, many other pastors were morally failing in some way—affairs, scandals, abuse, alcohol, lies, and more—all the while standing behind the most sacred place in the church—the pulpit—and telling people to trust God. Complete hypocrisy! People listened and put their trust in God, largely because they trusted that pastor. So, I understand the struggle to trust God when everything you once thought to be true was actually a lie.

HUMANS DO WHAT HUMANS HAVE ALWAYS DONE BEST: MESS THINGS UP AND MAKE MISTAKES.

Over the past couple of years, it has grieved me to watch the downfall of Hillsong and Gateway Church and the ripple effect it has had on the church, Christians, and non-Christians. The pain, the heartbreak, and the broken trust have impacted countless lives. I believe in restoration, and I trust it is at work in their lives. When leaders mess up, they should do whatever it takes to make things right with God and with those their actions have affected because they are held to a higher standard. When leaders take that step, it demonstrates the right way to handle trust issues and reminds everyone that restoration is possible for them. Unresolved hurt will grow without accountability or efforts at restoration, leading to even more trust issues. I rejoice when restoration happens because it offers healing to everyone. But let me pause here to speak to any and every pastor, leader, teacher, and parent. *How you live matters!* We'll get more into this in chapter 7, but you need to feel the weight of it now. Trust me when I tell you, you don't want to be the reason anyone says they don't trust God. It's in those moments I have to remind myself of the fallen world we live in and that everyone is human. Humans do what humans have always done best: mess things up and make mistakes. It started in the beginning and has continued to this day.

In fact, most of the heroes of the Bible that we look up to have all messed up. And before you say it, I am not justifying actions that may have directly affected you or given you trust issues. Sin is sin; wrong is wrong, and those who hurt you will be held accountable to God one day. Just don't forget that what's true for them is also true for you. I don't say that to scare you. No one likes to hear that everyone will be held accountable by God, but we should thank God for accountability—the only reason He brings sin to the surface and exposes it is because He loves us. We need to view accountability as His mercy and grace on our lives so that we all have the opportunity to make it to heaven. In fact, accountability draws you nearer to God and teaches you and others how to trust or keep trusting in Him.

My love for Zaxby's fried chicken lands me in that drive-thru window on a regular basis. I can't even tell you how many times they have made my order wrong, left out my sauces, forgotten the napkins, asked me to pull up to wait, and once even dropped a large, sweet tea in my truck, yet I still go back! I'm not going to let a few irritating experiences keep me from experiencing something I enjoy. Deciding not to trust God because someone failed you is like giving up on food altogether after one bad experience at a five-star restaurant. I'm begging you, *please don't blame God for somebody else's mistake, mess-up, or sin!*

THAT WASN'T GOD

You very well may blame your trust issues on God because you believe He allowed challenges to happen. So, the question is, how do you trust a God who you feel has let you down? Let's consider

Job for a moment. The Bible tells us that Job was extremely blessed by God and had become very wealthy in the process. God gave him a wife, seven sons, and three daughters, and he owned thousands and thousands of livestock. Job was loaded! Scripture also tells us that he was blameless, righteous, feared God, shunned evil, and that no one on earth was like him. He was doing everything right! Yet, the Lord allowed Satan to bring chaos to every part of his life.

> **GUARD YOUR HEART AND ALWAYS REMEMBER THAT PEOPLE CAN CAUSE YOUR TRUST ISSUES.**

When nothing could be better, out of nowhere, all of Job's livestock was killed, along with all his servants. On the same day, his children were together in one of the brothers' houses when it collapsed and killed them all. After he lost all his possessions and children, Job was struck with a terrible disease that caused him to suffer greatly. It got so bad that even his wife turned to him and said, "Are you still maintaining your integrity? Curse God and die!" (Job 2:9, NIV) In other words, "Stop trusting God and just give up!" If you're wondering, you don't run to someone like Job's wife for a prayer request when tragedy strikes. Let this be a lesson to you on how important it is to always have the right people in your corner. The people you allow in your life can influence you to turn to or turn away from God. They can encourage you and lift you up, or they can discourage you and pull you down. Guard your heart and always remember that people can cause your trust issues. The person Job should have been able to trust the most told him to stop trusting God! So, if anyone knew about trust issues, it was Job.

Did Job struggle? Absolutely! Did he question why God had let so much pain into his life? No doubt! Did Job speak out of line about where God was in all of this? Yeah! Long story short, Job had a one-on-one with God, and he soon realized that God was in control no matter what. So, he humbled himself before the Lord and continued to trust that God knew best. In turn, God blessed the latter part of Job's life more than the former. Trusting God will not always make sense, but it will always be what's best! *God has this extraordinary ability to take everything the enemy meant for your evil and turn it for your good! But you have to trust Him.*

I don't claim to have all the answers to your questions, but I do know a few things. Jesus told us in Matthew 5:45 (NLT, author addition) that "[God] gives his sunlight to both the evil and the good, and he sends rain on the just and the unjust alike." One thing this shows us is that life will be full of ups and downs, good and bad, joy and heartbreak, and rights and wrongs. At some point, every organization, institution, business, church, and person will probably disappoint you and/or hurt you. Ninety-nine percent of the time, their actions will be unintentional. The flat-out jerks you encounter from time to time make up the other 1 percent. Every situation is a good opportunity to practice forgiveness and extend grace so that bitterness doesn't take root in your heart. I don't mean to be rude or burst your bubble, but you're not perfect, either, and you've probably hurt someone before, causing their trust issues. Understand this: Forgiveness is for *you*, not the other person! Forgiveness allows you to live free of toxic emotions toward anyone, especially God and His church.

> **A LACK OF TRUST WILL CAUSE YOU TO MISS OUT ON THE BEST OF HEAVEN.**

Can I speak to you as an imperfect pastor? If someone in a church hurt you, that wasn't God! More than likely, it was a hurting person because hurting people hurt people. I don't say that to justify the wrong committed against you. It's just the truth. Please get back to church and place your trust in God. Don't blame Him and miss out on all the good He wants to do in your life because of someone else's poor judgment. A lack of trust will cause you to miss out on the best of heaven. Choose forgiveness and put your trust in God. Life is so much better that way! As a pastor, people hurt me all the time. It's the seat I have the honor of sitting in. I've been lied to, lied about, disrespected, wrongfully accused, betrayed, cursed at, and even had my life threatened, and I still show up! Why? Because I love God and believe in the local church.

Look at what church people did to Jesus. They hated Him, despised Him, falsely accused Him, and schemed against Him, but He never stopped showing up. They eventually killed Him, and even that didn't keep Him from showing back up! Jesus rose from the dead so that we could have new life! He is seated at the right hand of the Father, highly exalted above all forever. And now, because He conquered death and the grave, we get to experience victory in our lives too! In other words, if we will put our trust in Him, we will be victorious with Him.

If you've been hurt in life, take a good look around because God is near you. Psalm 34:18 (NLT) promises that "The LORD is close to the brokenhearted; he rescues those whose spirits are crushed." It's not an accident that you're reading this book. God wants to get your attention and tell you how much He loves you and that you really can trust Him! God wants to heal the hurt others have caused so that you can experience the power, peace, and blessing of trusting in Him! People will fail you and hurt you, but God never will! *News flash: You have trust issues because of people, not God!*

If you've been lied to . . . that wasn't God!
If you've been cheated on . . . that wasn't God!
If you've been abused . . . that wasn't God!
If you've been raped . . . that wasn't God!
If you've been betrayed . . . that wasn't God!
If you've been neglected . . . that wasn't God!
If you've been gossiped about . . . that wasn't God!
If you've been given up on . . . that wasn't God!
God didn't hurt you . . . that person did!
God didn't let you down . . . that organization dropped the ball!
God didn't mislead you . . . that was someone else!

> ## "WHY" WILL KEEP YOU STUCK, BUT "WHAT" WILL SET YOU FREE.

Through it all, no mishap, misfortune, or mess-up can stop God's promises for your life. It's really easy to throw your hands up at God and ask, "Why?" "Why did God allow that to happen to me?" "Why didn't God stop that person from hurting me?" But asking why can become a barrier to trusting Him. Please allow me to encourage you to *change your "why" to "what."*

"God, *what* are you trying to show me?"

"*What* are you trying to teach me?"

"*What* are you trying to give to me or keep me from?"

In other words, "what" is better than "why."

We didn't ask God why when someone lied to me in 2012. We asked Him what. Then, He showed us what needed to be done and took us down the right path that led to our breakthrough. "Why" will keep you stuck, but "what" will set you free. "Why" causes bitterness, but "what" leads to blessings and helps you to trust Him, even when it doesn't make sense to!

> ## I CAN TRUST SOMEONE WITHOUT PUTTING MY TRUST IN THEM.

Your heart needs healing before you can trust God again, or maybe even for the first time. Failing to get this right will negatively affect your whole outlook on life and even impact your relationships. When Louisa Stead lost her husband in 1880, her response had an eternal impact on not only her daughter but the entire world. As she continued to trust in God through the tragedy, He made a way to fulfill her desire to become a missionary! Her trust in God was so powerful that her daughter continued the work as a missionary long after she passed away. Through Louisa's struggle and tragedy, millions of lives have been encouraged and changed. She showed people that no matter what happens, God can be trusted. So, start asking Him "what," and learn to trust in Him. He won't let you down!

Psalm 146:3 (NIV) says, "Do not put your trust . . . in human beings, who cannot save." So, I can trust someone without putting my trust in them. I may trust someone to save me a seat, but I'm not going to trust them to save my life. If I trust someone without trusting *in* them, I can run to the One I DO put my trust in when they inevitably mess up or hurt me! That's JESUS! Proverbs 18:10 (NKJV) says, "The name of the LORD *is* a strong tower; The righteous run to it and are safe!"

When you get hurt . . . run to JESUS!
When your best friend lets you down . . . run to JESUS!
When your church disappoints you . . . run to JESUS!
When your marriage takes a hit . . . run to JESUS!
When your job mistreats you . . . run to JESUS!
When you get overlooked . . . run to JESUS!
When life rains on you . . . run to JESUS!

No matter what happens . . . keep running to JESUS, and never stop trusting Him!

HERE'S THE BIG IDEA:

God desires to bless you—never hurt you. Trust Him, even when it doesn't make any sense. He knows what He's doing in your life! He specializes in turning things around for your good!

CONSIDER:

- Do you fully trust God?
- Are you holding on to unforgiveness?

CHALLENGE:

- Address the source of your trust issues with God head-on. Don't run from them.
- Let go of bitterness and unforgiveness so you can live free and learn to trust again.
- Seek out advice from a pastor or Christian counselor.

PRAYER:

Heavenly Father,
I need You! Forgive me for the times that I blamed You for the pain in my life that other people caused. I need Your grace and forgiveness for my life, so I've decided today to forgive them for the wrong they caused me. Please help me with my trust issues. I choose to trust You no matter what happens in my life because I know that You are for me, with me, and will never leave me. I trust You! In Jesus's name. Amen!

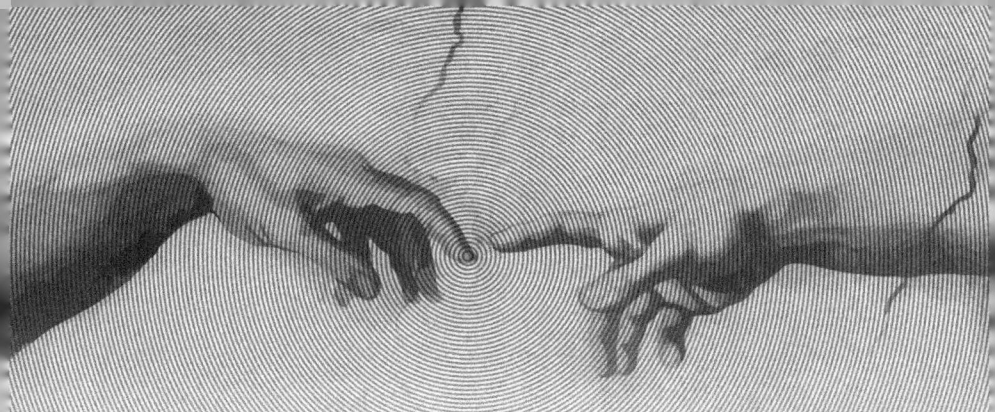

CHAPTER 4

HOLD FAST

IF **MATT CAHOON** can still put His trust in God, there's hope for you!

In 2019, Matt came home from work to find his pregnant wife, Sierra, and their son, Nolan, all ready for a walk. Matt knew it was about to storm, so he warned them to make it quick to avoid getting stuck out in the rain. He sat down to rest for a few minutes while they were gone, only to realize that way too much time had passed for things to be okay. Worried, he left to try and find them. After several failed attempts, he made one last trip down a different road, where he discovered a large commotion of emergency vehicles and officers. The closer he got, the more his heart raced and sank as he recognized some of the debris. Upon his arrival on the scene, Matt discovered that a man, with sick and evil intentions, purposely drove his vehicle at breakneck speed into his pregnant wife and precious son, killing them instantly. In one moment, Matt's entire world had been torn apart.

I will never forget the moment I walked into his apartment to find Matt sitting on the couch, staring at a blank TV screen and surrounded by a few of Nolan's toys on the floor. What do you say to someone whose pregnant wife was just tragically murdered? What do you say to a dad whose son was killed and had just celebrated Father's Day a few days prior? "Hey, man, just trust God!" Nope! In fact, that's the dumbest thing you could possibly say!

Matt and his family were brand new to our church, and we had not yet had the opportunity to establish a relationship with each other. So, walking in his place that day, the only thing I knew to do was to love him, cry with him, mourn with him, and let him know that I would do whatever he wanted and needed. I felt helpless because I couldn't give him the very thing he wanted and needed (his wife and kids). I have never told Matt this, but I decided that day the best thing I could do was to trust God *for* him.

After that day, our church, the community, and so many more did whatever we knew to do to help him pick up the broken pieces of his life. Honestly, I was so concerned about him and his faith. How do you bounce back from that? How do you trust God after your world has been shattered into that many pieces? Several days after the funeral, I asked Matt if he'd like to go out one night to grab some dinner and possibly catch a movie in hopes that his mind would rest and some joy might return to his heart. I asked him to select the restaurant and movie because it was his night to fully enjoy. *Toy Story 4* had just been released in the theaters, and I knew there was no way in the world he would ever choose it after what had happened to his son. But once we finished eating, I asked him what he'd like to watch, and his response completely caught me off guard.

"Nolan was so excited about *Toy Story 4*, so I'd like to go watch it."

I tried to swallow and just said, "Absolutely!" I can't even begin to tell you how honored I was to sit with this man in the movie theater as we laughed and cried through the whole thing. Throughout the movie, I prayed the entire time, *God, please help Matt! Give him strength to trust You as he walks through this pain.* Over the next several weeks, months, and years, I watched Matt fight his way through the heartbreak and have witnessed God work a miracle in his life. Recently, he agreed to let me ask him some really tough questions about how he got through the darkest times of his life. I asked, "How did you learn to put your trust in God again?" I could write a whole book on his answers, but I'll let him share all the details in his upcoming book. However, I will share some of his wisdom that I believe will help you with your trust issues.

Matt told me that on that horrific day, he felt like he had lost his past, his present, and his future all in one moment. His past was Sierra because they had been married for eight years but in a relationship for a total of thirteen; his present was Nolan, who was two years old at that time; his future was the precious baby inside Sierra's womb. He had lost it all.

He had many questions for God. "Where do I go from here? What in the world just happened to me? God, what did I do to deserve this? You're supposed to be my Heavenly Father! How could you let this happen?" They are all valid questions. Matt said that God never answered those questions, so he was left only with more questions. He said he was never angry with God but was extremely disappointed with Him. He thought, *I'm a father, and I would never allow this to happen to my son.* If God is our heavenly Father, shouldn't we be able to trust that He would never allow something like that to happen to one of His own? This is the question that runs through our minds and grips our hearts when we endure a tragedy or unfair situation. Surely, you can understand why Matt had trust issues! Just when he thought things couldn't get any worse, Matt hit his lowest of lows when he turned to other things to try to find fulfillment, peace, and relief. He turned to alcohol to try and numb the pain. He turned to pornography in hopes of filling the void. But he was left with more emptiness everywhere he turned. He found himself reaching for his Bible when he realized that something had to change. He asked, "Is God who He says He is in this book? Is this book truth? Do I throw it out? Or do I hold on tight and dive deeper into faith?" Matt decided to lean on the foundation that his parents raised him to build his life on, and he put his trust back in God.

In chapter 3, I said that we tend to ask the wrong question when we are drowning in trust issues. We ask "why" instead of "what." Slowly, Matt began to transition from "why" into "what." I watched as this man went on a journey to find healing and, somehow, make sense of everything that had happened to him. He prayed that God would lead him to find help, accountability, and people he could trust. Instead of asking all the questions that were getting him nowhere, he began to lean into "what" he would need to heal. I asked him what he did to heal and what advice he had for you, and his answer was two words: "Find community." He got more involved at church with our life groups and started serving on a Dream Team. Matt found a community that has changed his life and brought clarity to his trust issues.

"WHAT" # 1: FIND COMMUNITY

In the Bible, Matthew, Mark, and Luke write about the forgiveness and healing of a paralytic man. We don't know his name or anything about him other than the fact that he was paralyzed. Jesus had become very well-known because of His teaching and the miracles He had performed. The news spread as people from Galilee, Judea, and Jerusalem came to witness Jesus for themselves. In all three accounts of this story, so many people were gathered that no one else could get inside where Jesus was to hear His teachings or see His miracles.

> **FEELING LIKE YOU CAN'T TRUST GOD CAN LEAVE YOU STUCK AND SPIRITUALLY PARALYZED. SOMETIMES, YOU NEED TO LEAN ON COMMUNITY AND BORROW THEIR FAITH!**

Four men noticed a paralyzed man who needed healing, so they carried him on a mat onto the top of the house. There, they tore apart the roof so they could lower the man down to Jesus. (Can anyone tell me why the owner of this house didn't care that someone was tearing their roof off? I guess what Jesus was doing in that community was so life-changing that nothing else mattered!)

They lowered him down to Jesus, and He forgave the paralyzed man's sins and then healed him. This man stood up, picked up his mat, and went home praising God because he had been healed! Now, Matthew, Mark, and Luke all make a statement that will blow your mind: "When Jesus saw their faith," *then* he forgave the man and healed him. Not the paralyzed man's faith, but their faith! This paralyzed man borrowed their faith, and it forever changed his life! (See Matthew 9:1-8; Mark 2:1-12; Luke 5:17-26.) *Your connections will determine your destiny.*

Feeling like you can't trust God can leave you stuck and spiritually paralyzed. Sometimes, you need to lean on community and borrow their faith! It was the faith of Matt's community that helped him find healing. He learned to borrow their faith. He was struggling to believe, but he knew the community believed. He was weak and tired spiritually, but he knew that the community had some strength. He was lonely and afraid, but he knew the community would provide relationship and comfort. He was struggling to connect to God through prayer, but he knew the community would help lift him up.

A community of faith is a strong force. He found himself at the altar Sunday after Sunday, worshiping God with them. He found himself week after week doing life and serving with them. It was their faith that lifted him up. As he learned to trust in their faith, his trust in God began to strengthen once again. In other words, a strong community will help you deal with your trust issues!

It's time for you to check your connections! Whom and what are you connected to? Your connections will determine your destiny. If you need to build your faith and/or need help with your trust issues, you have to surround yourself with the right community. You need some godly people of strong faith who will lift you up when you're down. People who will encourage you and let you lean on them. People who will cry with you and pray for you. People who will laugh and talk *with* you but never *about* you. *You need a community that will let you borrow their faith until you can trust again.*

As a pastor, I cannot even tell you how many times people have connected to our church, only to drift away until they hit a rough patch; then, they call me or come back. That's definitely not a cheap shot or knock on them. I'm simply saying that once you learn that godly people in the church are the only people who will help connect you with God, that's where you'll turn in times of need. You might be thinking, *I need a community like that. I need what Matt experienced.* If that's you, then I'm begging you to find a church or get back into church where you can find community and get connected to hope, where you can find fulfillment that will only come through God.

> **THE PATHWAY TO STRENGTH, COMFORT, HOPE, HEALING, RESTORATION, AND PEACE COMES FROM COMMUNITY.**

Moses had a great community, even though they sometimes did awful things and let him down. Never forget that people will do that from time to time, and so will you, but it was that same community that helped him fulfill God's purpose for his life. In fact, Moses's father-in-law, Jethro, came out to visit him one day while he was leading millions through the desert to follow God's instructions to the Promised Land. Moses was trying to meet with every single person, day in and day out, to help solve their problems. Jethro noticed his burden and helped him raise up a community of people who would assist him in leading the Israelites. It was a brilliant idea then, and it's still the best leadership model in the world today. That all came through a community. The pathway to strength, comfort, hope, healing, restoration, and peace comes from community. Ecclesiastes 4:9-12 (NIV) says:

> Two are better than one, because they have a good return for their labor. If either of them falls down, one can help the other up. But pity anyone who falls and has no one to help them up. Also, if two lie down together, they will keep warm. But how can one keep warm alone? Though one may be overpowered, two can defend themselves. A cord of three strands is not quickly broken.

Find a community because they will help you with all your trust issues!

"WHAT" #2: GET A GRIP

HOLD FAST. Throughout history, these two words are what some military sailors have tattooed on their knuckles as a reminder to never let go of the rope. They did this in hopes of extra motivation while working alongside their crew. As they gripped the rig, seeing "HOLD FAST" would remind them of just how important it was to push through the pain. If they let go, other people's lives would have been affected. It helped them realize that they could do anything for a little while and that the pain they were experiencing was only temporary. Holding fast was, and still is, always worth it.

The summer of 2012 through the spring of 2013 was the most challenging year of my life. I had to work in a factory to provide for my family financially the year we moved to Tennessee to launch The Avenue Church. Working at the factory wasn't what made that year so challenging. I would leave the house around 6:30 in the morning and then arrive back home around 7:30 in the evening. We would put our kids to bed around 8:30, and then Melissa and I would begin church work. When we weren't working on things together, I was up late studying and preparing the sermon for Sunday. There were many nights and weeks where I only got an hour or two of sleep each night. During that season of my life, I felt like I rarely saw the kids, and I was running on fumes. I love to work, but there are only so many hours in a day, and I was getting tired. It was one of the most exciting times of our lives—and also one of the most exhausting.

I remember my alarm going off one morning after what felt like only a few minutes of sleep. I sat on the edge of my bed and said to myself, "Hold fast; I can do anything for a little while." I thought about my wife and our kids, who were still asleep. I thought about the people who were already coming to church and those I was still praying and hoping would. I reminded myself that the season we were in would be worth it, and I would whisper to God, "I trust you." It was through this challenging season that God would teach us some of the most amazing lessons that are invaluable to us today. It was only temporary, and we simply had to trust God through it.

> # GOD WILL NEVER HURT YOU, AND HEAVEN WILL NEVER DISAPPOINT YOU.

When I sat down with Matt, I asked him where he was in the process of healing and trusting God. He answered that with a question for me. In 2010, I had torn the labrum in my shoulder. In 2018, I had snapped my bicep, and it curled up to my shoulder. After both of those surgeries, I did intense therapy to continue the healing, and with time, I got stronger and stronger. In fact, that shoulder and bicep feel stronger than my other shoulder and bicep today. Matt knew about these surgeries and asked, "Even though you're healed, I bet from time to time you feel a random pain, don't you?" He's right, I do. And the same goes for him. From time to time, something will trigger him, and he'll experience some pain, but it's nothing like it was. He had to learn how to hold fast and never let go of the promise of God's Word so that he could re-establish his trust in God through the temporary pain.

Matt explained how he had to totally shift his perspective. Through this process, God has helped him move his perspective from an earthly (temporary) perspective to a heavenly (eternal) perspective. Everything in this world had let him down. People let him down. Even the judicial system let him down—proper justice had not been served for the murder of his wife and kids. In the middle of pain, he grabbed hold of the Word of God and decided to trust Him with everything, and I encourage you to do the same with anything and everything you may be facing right now in your life. Hold fast, and don't let go! This world will hurt you, disappoint you, cause you pain, and leave you with so many questions, but not God, and not heaven. God will never hurt you, and heaven will never disappoint you. The earthly perspective will leave you with so many questions, but with a heavenly perspective, you'll realize that you already have the answers. In the Bible, Jesus said in John 16:33 (NLT), "Here on earth you will have many trials and sorrows. But take heart, because I have overcome the world." You can have hope to overcome the pains of this world and trust God because of Jesus! *Jesus is the Healer of all trust issues!*

THERE ARE NO SHORTCUTS TO TRUST. IT'S A JOURNEY!

As you're reading this book, you might be hoping for a quick fix to all your trust issues. That doesn't exist! There are no shortcuts to trust. It's a journey! Even if there were, you wouldn't want to take it because you'd miss out on everything there is to learn through the process. However, there *is* a solution to healing your trust issues with God: *Hold fast to hope, and don't let go!*

Hebrews 6:18-19 (NLT) says:

> *So God has given both his promise and his oath. These two things are unchangeable because it is impossible for God to lie. Therefore, we who have fled to him for refuge can have great confidence as we hold to the hope that lies before us. This hope is a strong and trustworthy anchor for our souls.*

ELPIS IS A DEEP ASSURANCE AND A FIRM CONFIDENCE THAT GOD CAN HANDLE THE HIGHEST OF HIGHS AND THE LOWEST OF LOWS.

I need you to see that this "hope" is "trustworthy." In Romans 15:13 (NLT), Paul said, "I pray that God, the source of hope, will fill you completely with joy and peace because you trust in him. Then you will overflow with confident hope through the power of the Holy Spirit." I need you to see the benefit of "trusting" in this "hope." The Greek word used here for "hope" is *elpis*. It means "assurance, security, expectation, confidence."[5] It's not the weak concept of wishful thinking. *Elpis* is a deep assurance and a firm

---

5   *Logos Bible Software,* s.v. "elips," accessed April 8, 2025, https://www.logos.com/.

confidence that God can handle the highest of highs and the lowest of lows. *Elpis* is what helped Matt Cahoon trust in God again, and *elpis* is what will help you, too!

Let me help bring some clarity to why holding on to *elpis* is so awesome. Paul said in 1 Timothy 1:1 that Christ Jesus is our hope. *Jesus is Elpis!* That *Hope* is the solution to all your trust issues. It's not that easy, but it is that simple. Always remember, *'Tis so sweet to trust in Jesus.* Allow me to give you one more scripture. Paul said in Ephesians 1:18 (NIV), "I pray that the eyes of your heart may be enlightened in order that you may know the hope to which he has called you, the riches of his glorious inheritance in his holy people." This hope is all about the riches He desires to give us as an inheritance—the treasures that God has ready and available for us. In other words, everything that heaven offers is available to anyone who puts their hope in Jesus! If heaven has it, then you can have it. *News flash: You will find joy and peace when you hold fast and trust in Jesus!* When you place your hope and trust in Jesus, you will have more than enough to overcome anything and everything this world throws at you.

When you trust in God . . . you will receive strength in your weakness!

When you trust in God . . . you will experience joy in the middle of sorrow!

When you trust in God . . . you find healing after the hurt and the pain!

When you trust in God . . . you will encounter comfort even in the chaos!

When you trust in God . . . you won't need all the answers because you'll have the assurance and confidence that God is in control!

I declare God's Word over you right now, even as you read this. Your life is about to overflow with confident hope and fill you with victory, joy, and peace as you take a step of faith and hold fast to hope! All of heaven is available to you if you will put your trust in God. Everything in this world may have let you down, but that's not God—He will never fail you. Change your perspective. Whatever you're experiencing right now is only temporary. If you find yourself in the valley, keep walking! If you find yourself in the dark, keep walking! If you find yourself in the desert, keep walking! If you find yourself in the heartbreak, keep walking! Even though sorrow may last for a season, it's only temporary. Joy is coming! Victory is coming! Breakthrough is coming! The hope of Jesus will help you overcome every trust issue you may have.

> **THE SOLUTION TO ALL YOUR TRUST ISSUES WITH GOD IS FOUND IN KNOWING THE SAVIOR OF THE WORLD, AND HIS NAME IS JESUS!**

No matter what mountain you may be facing in your life right now, stop seeking the answers to all your "why" questions. Simply trust in the One who is more than able to work everything out. Trust in God with your marriage. Trust in God with your finances. Trust in God with your children. Trust in God with your future. Trust in God with your church. Trust in God with your health.

Trust in God to help you overcome the pain, the addiction, the hurt, the fear, the depression, the unforgiveness, the anxiety, or anything else that's causing you issues. He can handle it all way better than you can, and to top it off, you can be at peace that He's going to work it all for your good!

By the way, Matt is doing better than ever because he decided to deal with his trust issues. He shared how he is, without a doubt, closer to God than he's ever been. His faith is stronger because he decided to hold fast and not let go of Hope. I watched God do what He does best: perform miracles. God brought an amazing woman (Mandi) along with her two beautiful girls into his life, and they married in 2021. In 2024, Mandi gave birth to another precious daughter. However, you must understand that this is not Matt's redemption story, and it definitely doesn't replace those he lost. Matt's family is an addition to the redemption he already has in Jesus! The same applies to you. The answer you're looking for is in Jesus. The victory you're longing for is in Jesus. The solution to all your trust issues with God is found in knowing the Savior of the world, and His name is Jesus! While we can always count on God to be trustworthy, the question we have to ask ourselves is . . . can He count on us?

HERE'S THE BIG IDEA:

No matter what this world has thrown your way, find community and trust in God. If you hold on to the Hope—Jesus—He will lead you through every storm and trial, drawing you closer to God than you ever thought possible!

CONSIDER:

- Have there been any traumas in your life that have given you trust issues?
- Are you connected to a faith community through a local church?

CHALLENGE:

- Join a class or small group in your church to get connected and volunteer with other people.
- Start or keep praying and reading the Bible every day, so you can find the strength to continue your walk through this season of life.

PRAYER:

Heavenly Father,
You are everything I need, both now and forever. I'm choosing to trust You with my life. Help me to release the control over to You. Will You please lead me to the right people who will help with my trust issues? Give me strength to hold fast and never let go of Hope! I know that I can do all things through Christ who gives me that strength. In Jesus's name. Amen!

PART 2

CAN GOD TRUST YOU?

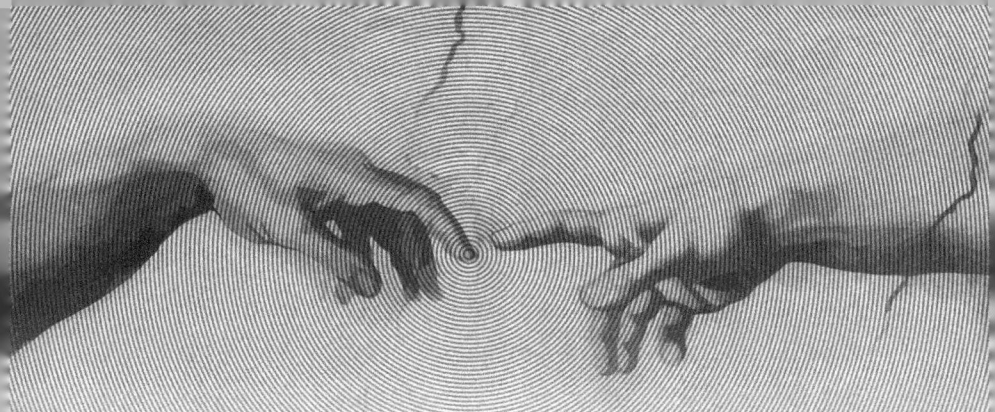

CHAPTER 5

DON'T TAKE
THE BAIT

I **AM DEFINITELY NOT** a skilled fisherman, but one day I caught
over a hundred fish in just a couple of hours. One summer evening in Americus, Georgia, when I was just a kid, my family and
I went to one of our friends' lake houses and fished off their dock.
I had only been fishing a few times before and knew it could be a
long waiting game and a test of your patience. This night spared us
that test. We had several poles and a bag full of bread as our bait.
My uncle instructed us kids to simply ball up some bread for bait,
shove it on the hook, and cast it out into the lake. To my surprise,
fish were biting as soon as the bait hit the water. We caught fish
as fast as we could get the bait on the line and into the water. For
whatever reason, those fish loved the bread we were using as bait.
Fish after fish led to buckets filled with bluegill. I don't remember
every detail of that evening, but it was mind-blowing! (I'll confess
that I had some help catching over a hundred fish, but it sounds
better when I take all the credit.) Our large family and friends
knew how to do things right. So, we brought out some deep fryers
and had ourselves a good old-fashioned fish fry!

To this day, I really enjoy fishing, but only with people who know what they're doing because, after all these years, I still can't seem to figure out how to be a successful fisherman. I have embarrassed myself one too many times with my own kids. On one particular excursion, I caught a fish so small that my kids used it as bait to catch a bigger one. So, I only go fishing with guys who basically boss me around and tell me what to do. In fact, several men in our church are really good at fishing. One of those guys recently took me out on his boat to enjoy a summer evening on one of the beautiful lakes in East Tennessee. We didn't go out just to see if we could catch something. We went out on a mission to find specific types of fish.

We drove to different spots because the location, the depth, and the fish would determine what kind of bait we would put on our hooks. Taking things to another level, he had a fishing sonar that showed us exactly where the fish were. I saw my line go down and watched the fish charge at the bait. It was like playing a video game with this technology—those fish had no chance! They took the bait left and right, so I felt like I actually knew what I was doing. Spoiler alert: I still have no clue! We had tools and tricks that the fish couldn't outsmart. Likewise, Satan and his crew have tricks up their sleeves to try and outsmart us. The good news is that he has no new tricks. We just have to learn to stop falling for them and refuse to take the bait.

HELL'S BAIT

Jesus's brother gave us some incredible God-given wisdom to help us with our trust issues. In James 1:12-15 (NIV), he wrote:

Blessed is the one who perseveres under trial because, having stood the test, that person will receive the crown of life that the Lord has promised to those who love him. When tempted, no one should say, "God is tempting me." For God cannot be tempted by evil, nor does he tempt anyone; but each person is tempted when they are dragged away by their own evil desire and enticed. Then, after desire has conceived, it gives birth to sin; and sin, when it is full-grown, gives birth to death.

James used two different important "T" words we can use to examine our trust issues. The word "trial" used here in Greek is *peirasmos*. It simply means "test."[6]

> ## TRIALS ARE TESTS THAT WILL BUILD YOUR TRUST IN GOD. TEMPTATIONS ARE TESTS THAT REVEAL WHETHER GOD CAN TRUST YOU!

James talks about trials in verses 1-11 of that same chapter, explaining how they actually strengthen your faith and develop perseverance. But when James gets to verse 13, he flips the script a little and starts talking about being tempted. The word "tempted" used here in Greek is *peirazō*. It means "test, to try to trap, to attempt to catch in a mistake."[7] At first glance, these two words

---

6   *Logos Bible Software*, s.v. "peirasmos" accessed April 29, 2025, https://www.logos.com/.
7   *Logos Bible Software*, s.v. "peirazō" accessed April 29, 2025, https://www.logos.com/.

seem very similar, but they are definitely not the same. James is identifying different *types* of tests that you will experience in this life, and both of them will impact your trust issues.

A trial is a test that God allows for the purpose of strengthening your faith. A temptation is a test that Satan uses to weaken your faith! It's imperative that you understand the difference. Trials are tests that will build your trust in God. Temptations are tests that reveal whether God can trust you! God allows trials to build your trust in Him, but the enemy of your faith uses temptations to lure you into sin so that God won't trust you. God will allow trials, but He will never tempt you! God is the One you can trust through the trial, and He's also the One who will help you overcome any and every temptation so you can build trust!

Please get this next part because it will set the tone for the rest of this book. James said in verse 14 that "each person is tempted when they are dragged away by their own evil desire and enticed." The word *enticed* used here in Greek is *deleazō*. It means "to lure, catch by a bait."[8] Different bait is used for different types of fish because it's been proven effective through testing. If you want to catch bluegill, you change the bait. If you want to catch bass, you change the bait. So, James is warning us that hell sees you like fish. Satan's ultimate goal is to destroy your life. He wants to lure you in and catch you with his bait so you'll make decisions that will ruin your life and destroy trust. He wants to ruin your trust in God and get you to mess up so God will never trust you. Hell wants you to have many trust issues!

---

8   *Logos Bible Software*, s.v. "deleazō" accessed April 29, 2025, https://www.logos.com/.

TAKING BAIT BREAKS TRUST

Growing up, I'm pretty sure I played every sport offered. My favorites were basketball, baseball, football, and cross country. For several years, I even played travel soccer, but only up through middle school. In sixth grade, I became pretty good friends with another boy at school who was on my soccer team. We had a weekend tournament scheduled, so he invited me to spend the night at his house that Friday, and we carpooled together to and from our games. I can't recall all the details from that weekend, and I couldn't even tell you if we won or lost. (I'll just say we won because it makes me feel better about my early soccer career.) However, I do remember something that happened that made me struggle for many years.

My friend and I went back to his house to rest for a couple of hours in between our tournament games. While we were there, he said to me, "Come here, I want to show you something." We snuck into his parents' room, where he pulled out a *Playboy* magazine that his dad kept hidden. When he opened it, let's just say its contents shocked me. I was completely caught off guard because I had no idea something like that existed, and it opened up a world I was not ready for. As a young boy, I went home with a racing mind as I dealt with the conviction of the Holy Spirit. Even though I was only eleven years old, I knew in my heart that I shouldn't be involved in that. Unfortunately, I chose to take the bait that Satan offered, and as a result, I struggled with pornography for several years. That's embarrassing, and I'm definitely not proud of that part of my life. When temptation presented itself, I took the bait. I wondered if God still loved me and if I could ever be a trustworthy

JUSTIN GRAHAM

man of integrity. I had to work through a lot of shame to get to where I am today, which we will dive into in the next chapter.

STOP GIVING HELL CREDIT

If you study the Bible, you will learn that God is omnipotent, omniscient, and omnipresent. That means He is all-powerful, all-knowing, and everywhere at all times. It's incredible when you wrap your mind around that truth. God is awesome! On the flip side, Satan, the enemy of our faith, is not. His power is limited; he doesn't know everything, and he can't be in two places at once. In other words, God knows everything about you—even without you saying a word—because He created you and sees everything that happens in your life. He knows you better than you know yourself. Satan does not. The only knowledge that Satan has about you is the information you give him. He cannot read your mind, and he doesn't know your thoughts. However, he does want to ruin your life and give you severe trust issues. So, like a fisherman, he will cast out bait to see what you like, and the only way he knows your weaknesses and where you are easily tempted is when you take the bait!

> **HELL IS BEST AT MAKING SIN LOOK ATTRACTIVE SO THAT YOU'LL TAKE THE BAIT AND SEVER TRUST BETWEEN YOU AND GOD. THE ATTRACTION TO SIN IS HELL'S BAIT.**

Hell didn't know that you would struggle with alcohol until you took the bait of drinking with friends. Hell didn't know that you would struggle with sexual purity until you took the bait of pornography or sex outside of marriage. Hell didn't know that you would struggle with honesty until you took the bait of lying to see how it could benefit you financially and professionally. By "taking the bait," I mean any and every type of sin that Satan will use to entice you in hopes of ruining your life. Bait is what you see online or in a movie. Bait is what you hear in a song that causes your mind to wonder. It's the flirting co-worker. It's the gossip you read on social media. It's the comparison trap of success. It's the money that you think leads to happiness. It's the late night out with the wrong crowd. However, even good things can become bait. If Satan can't use evil things against you, he will use blessings to try and pull you away from God and His plan for your life. He will take what's working for you and try to turn it against you. For example, hell will even use the comfort of your own bed—your place of rest—against you on a Sunday morning when you know you really need to be in church. So, when you decide to sleep in instead of worshiping in God's house with God's people, you've taken his bait. And before you realize it, Satan begins to throw that same bait out there, hoping you will develop the bad habit of skipping church. No matter the bait he uses, his goal is to disconnect you from God.

There is a long list of different types of bait that hell will use against you. What I need you to understand is this: Hell is best at making sin look attractive so that you'll take the bait and sever trust between you and God. The attraction to sin is hell's bait.

The problem is that sin will take you further than you want to go. It will cost you more than you want to pay. It will keep you longer than you want to stay. And then all of hell will laugh at you when you take the bait! *So, the question is, what bait are you biting that keeps you in the miserable cycle of sin?* I know it can be frustrating because the same bait may have caught you over and over again, just like a fish. You're frustrated because you're feeding your own evil desires instead of leaning into Jesus. It's not that the enemy of your faith has an upper hand on you; it's that you keep revealing your wrong appetites to him, and every time you take the bait, hell comes back with more. At some point, you're going to have to wise up and stop taking the bait! You're stronger and better than that! You were created for so much more, so stop taking hell's bait—it does nothing but cause you pain, heartache, misery, and trust issues!

> **IT'S TIME TO DESTROY YOUR EXCUSES FOR TAKING THE BAIT AND BREAKING YOUR TRUST WITH GOD.**

The apostle Peter wrote in 1 Peter 5:8 (NIV), "Be alert and of sober mind. Your enemy the devil prowls around like a roaring lion looking for someone to devour." That scripture can sound very intimidating when you first read it. But there's a word in there that should give you confidence to overcome every temptation that will ever be placed in front of you. He said that the devil prowls around "like" a roaring lion. He is not a roaring lion! There is only One with that title, and His name is JESUS, the Lion from the tribe of Judah! Peter then says in verse 9: "Resist him, standing firm in the faith." In other words, the solution to defeating the enemy is to stop taking hell's bait and lean into Jesus!

EXCUSES HINDER TRUST

In 1 Corinthians 10:12-13 (NIV), Paul wrote:

> *So, if you think you are standing firm, be careful that you don't fall! No temptation has overtaken you except what is common to mankind. And God is faithful; he will not let you be tempted beyond what you can bear. But when you are tempted, he will also provide a way out so that you can endure it.*

No bait from hell exists that God hasn't already provided a way for you to overcome. Remember, trials are tests that will build your trust in God. Temptations are tests that reveal if God can trust you. So, every time you don't take the way out that God has provided, you're taking the bait, and you're ruining trust. No, the devil didn't cause you to sin. You took the bait! No, the devil didn't make you lose your temper and act a fool. You took the bait! No, the devil didn't cause you to cuss out your co-worker or teammate. You took the bait! No, the devil didn't take over your fingers and force you to post that ridiculous rant on social media. You took the bait! It's time to destroy your excuses for taking the bait and breaking your trust with God. Just like Moses, God is looking for people whom He can trust. Can He find that in you?

When Moses was leading the Israelites through the desert, he ran into some situations that would create trust issues for anyone. A short time into their journey, God called Moses up a mountain to spend time with Him and gave him instructions and laws for the people to live by. While he was gone, he left his brother, Aaron, in charge. The people became restless and wanted Aaron to make them gods because it seemed to them that Moses was not coming back. So, Aaron had them bring him some of their gold so he could fashion it with a tool to make a golden calf that would be their god. God was ticked over what was going on and sent Moses back down the mountain to deal with the situation. When Moses confronted Aaron, his excuse was that a golden calf popped out on its own when he threw their gold into the fire! Now that's a lame and pathetic excuse! Talk about trust issues. How could Moses truly trust his brother who responded to accountability this way? Excuses will always hinder trust. Just like Moses had to confront excuses head-on, I found myself face-to-face with a similar challenge on a basketball court in the fifth grade.

EXCUSES WILL ONLY KEEP YOU DEFEATED!

Growing up, I played basketball from preschool through high school. I wanted to be like the GOAT, aka Michael Jordan. The only problem with that is that I only grew to 6'1", and I'm White.

No one was dunking in the fifth grade anyway, so it was okay. I played for my elementary school team, the Manley Eagles. Our coach, Mr. Ralph Livesay, was also our principal. We had a really successful regular season, which landed us the #1 seed going into the tournament. So, obviously, we played the worst-seeded team of the year in the first round. We had played this team twice in the regular season and smoked them both times. We thought we were awesome. Although no one said it, we thought defeating them to kick off the tournament would be easy. To our shock, they came out guns blazing in the first half and were beating us by halftime. We were stunned in the locker room, and that's when Coach Livesay came in hot like a man on fire. At least that's how it felt. During his heated talk, he singled me out and said something to me that I will never forget. "Graham, where are you tonight? You're the biggest reason why we're getting our butts whooped! Wherever he is, you need to find him because your team needs him!" Big tears started swelling up in my eyes, and one or two may have made their way down my face, but I was hoping you couldn't tell with all the sweat. I got so mad at him!

At first, I started thinking about how poorly some of the other guys on the team were playing. I started making excuses for why it wasn't just my fault. But then something clicked, and I said to myself, *I'll show him that I'm here!* I know it was just elementary basketball, but at the moment, it felt like the NBA championship final was on the line. I came out in the second half like a madman, and we fought our way back and won by more than twenty points! We had a leader we trusted who didn't leave room for excuses.

Coach Livesay made such a significant impact on my life, and I honor and respect him greatly.

News flash: It's time to destroy the excuses for why you keep taking the bait. Excuses will only keep you defeated! Excuses will keep you stuck in the same frustrating sin cycle. You must take ownership of your own mistakes! You might find yourself frustrated with where you are in life, and you have allowed hell to convince you that your misery is all God's fault or someone else's. You might even be upset with God, and you're finding it hard to trust Him. But maybe YOU are the real issue! Allow me to call you out the same way Coach Livesay called me out that night because I care for you enough to tell you that you may be the reason for the trust issues between you and God. You've been taking the bait instead of taking the way out of temptation! You have allowed your own desire to sin to drag you away. How do you expect God to bless your life when you're too busy taking the bait? How do you expect God to bless your marriage when you're too busy taking the bait of adultery and dishonesty? How do you expect God to bless your finances when you're too caught up with taking the bait of bad stewardship? How do you expect God to bless your future when you're not being faithful to Him now? *God can't bless you if you keep making excuses for why you're taking the bait!* Excuses will keep you stuck in the trap of constantly biting hell's bait.

I love You, God, and I want to earn Your trust, but I'd rather take hell's bait!

I love You, God, but I'd rather continue my secret pornography habit!

I love You, God, but I'm going to continue abusing my family!

I love You, God, but I'm going to keep neglecting prayer, the Bible, and the church!

I love You, God, but I'm going to keep drinking when I get off work!

I love You, God, but I'm going to keep hiding that sin from You!

I love You, God, but this is just who I am!

I love You . . . but I'm gonna keep taking the bait!

It's time to get gut-wrenchingly honest with yourself and God. I had to, and I'm so glad I did. I want to answer God with an unwavering "Yes!" when He asks, "Can I trust you?" and I want the same for you. But, if you continue to take the bait, you'll cause trust issues. When you keep returning to that sin that I know you want and need to be freed from, you're causing trust issues! When you allow yourself to be dragged away and enticed, you're causing trust issues! Then, when things don't go the way you had hoped, you throw your hands up at God and complain to others about your trust issues!

WITH ANY AND EVERY TEMPTATION, PAY ATTENTION TO WHO'S HOLDING THE FISHING ROD!

Right now, in this very moment, as you're reading this book, it's time to stop taking the bait, stop blaming God, and start living right to gain His trust! You can do this! Don't give the devil the satisfaction of thinking his plans against you will defeat you.

With any and every temptation, pay attention to who's holding the fishing rod! Resist him, and don't take the bait! Jesus said in John 10:10 (NKJV) that "the thief does not come except to steal, and to kill, and to destroy. I have come that they may have life, and that they may have it more abundantly." The reality is that hell is against you. The good news is that all of heaven is for you! And Jesus wants to help you live this life in such a way as to gain God's trust. Having God's trust is extremely valuable and life-changing. There are blessings, favors, and miracles just waiting for you when you gain God's trust. Can God trust you?

The more you avoid hell's bait, the more trust you earn from God! In your own strength, this seems nearly impossible. No matter where you stand with God today, there's hope! If you become a person of prayer and make the commitment to read the Bible and apply it to your life, you won't be hungry for hell's bait! The more you lean into Jesus and His Word, the more you will learn to trust Him through every trial and gain the strength to overcome every temptation. As a result, you will begin to earn God's trust!

HERE'S THE BIG IDEA:

Don't take the bait because it's never worth it. There's nothing that hell can offer you that can compare to God's blessings! Destroy excuses and start gaining God's trust!

CONSIDER:
- What bait (sin) have you been taking that's causing frustration and trust issues?
- What excuses do you give to justify your actions?

CHALLENGE:

- Take time each day to read and apply the Bible to your life.
- Take time to pray each day, asking God to show you the way out so that you may overcome temptation.
- Reach out to your pastor or your leader at church to seek out accountability.

PRAYER:

Heavenly Father,

Forgive me for all the times that I have taken the bait and held onto excuses that only enabled me to continue living in sin. I have no one to blame but myself, and I want to earn Your trust. Help me see the way out of every temptation so I don't get caught back up in that sin cycle. Thank You for your grace and mercy and for being so patient with me. Thank You for allowing me to be honest with You and the One whom I can always trust! Help me to live in such a way that brings honor to You. In Jesus's name. Amen!

CHAPTER 6

SHAME ON YOU

FAILURE. **LOSER. DISAPPOINTMENT.** Embarrassment. Unqualified. Hypocrite. Shameful. Every single time I think back to moments when I took the bait, these are the words that flood my heart and mind. To this very day, when I drive by the *Playboy* magazine house, I battle a flood of emotions. There have been times I've even gone a different route just to avoid going down memory lane. It's crazy how one reminder of taking hell's bait can open up an entire memory highway of shameful moments. Driving by that house reminds me of the seasons when I struggled with shame and pornography. So, when God has asked me, "Can I trust you?" I have struggled to answer Him with a "yes" because of the times that I've taken the bait! Before you judge me and say, "Shame on you!" please be careful and just hear me out.

Let's go back to Moses. He was born in an extremely hostile time. God had blessed the Israelites in Egypt in an incredible way, and they were multiplying at a very fast pace. Pharaoh became afraid and made a disgusting and evil decision to kill all the newborn Israelite males to diminish their population. But God's hand was on Moses, and in faith, his mother placed him in a basket to float him down the Nile River in hopes that God would protect him and spare his life.

Long story short, Pharaoh's family discovered Moses and raised him as their own. For forty years, Moses grew up and lived with Pharaoh in the palace like an Egyptian. Somewhere along the line, Moses understood that he was actually an Israelite and realized that his people were in slavery and were being treated poorly. One day, he noticed an Egyptian beating one of his fellow Israelites and decided to take matters into his own hands. Moses killed that Egyptian, buried him in the sand, and hoped that no one would find out. The very next day, two other Israelites informed Moses that they knew he had killed the Egyptian man. Pharaoh found out about it and tried to kill him. Moses was afraid for his life and ran away from Egypt to live in the desert. Talk about shame. Moses was a fugitive on the run, had abandoned his own people, and was a murderer!

Yet, in Numbers 12:7 (NLT, author addition), God said, "Of all my house, [Moses] is the one I trust." Moses? Really? How? He should be in prison! Moses was a failure. He was an embarrassment. He disqualified himself. What he did was absolutely shameful! He killed a man! When Moses ran away from Egypt, he spent the next forty years in the backside of the wilderness as a shepherd. It was there in the desert that God showed up in the burning bush and told Moses to go back to Egypt to set the Israelites free from bondage and slavery. Can you imagine the flood of emotions and thoughts? Can you imagine the guilt and shame that he must have felt? In fact, Moses was so overwhelmed with shame that he gave five excuses to convince God to use somebody else.

THOSE WERE THE DAYS . . . RIGHT?

The older I get, the more I hear people say, "Those were the days!" when they remember some of the good things in the past and compare them to the present. I am a child of the eighties and a teenager of the nineties. When I look back, I think about Nintendo, Super Mario, Ralphy the pink Christmas bunny, Blockbuster and VHS tapes, arcade games, Michael Jordan, *Rocky*,[9] and *Back to the Future*.[10] The eighties and nineties remind me of Journey, Michael Jackson, Whitney Houston, Nirvana, Outkast, Biggie Smalls, and Tupac. I've watched every episode, multiple times, of *Saved by the Bell*[11] and *The Fresh Prince of Bel-Air*.[12] Those were the days!

Maybe a different decade or time reminds you of the "good ole days." Whenever that time may be, it produces nostalgia, defined as "a wistful (longing) or excessively sentimental yearning (desire) for return to some past period or irrecoverable condition."[13] Nostalgia is a "longing for or thinking fondly of a past time or condition." It's why we can't wait to watch the same Christmas movies that we've seen a billion times. It's also why some people don't like change. If you change something, you run the risk of taking away

9   Sylvester Stallone, *Rocky* (1976-2006; Los Angeles, CA: 20th Century Studios).
10   Robert Zemeckis, *Back to the Future* (July 3, 1985; Universal City, CA: Universal Pictures).
11   *Saved by the Bell*, Sam Bobrick (August 20, 1989; New York, NY: Peter Engel Productions and NBC Productions), Television.
12   *The Fresh Prince of Bel-Air*, Andy Borowitz and Susan Borowitz (September 10, 1990; New York, NY: NBC Productions), Television.
13   *Merriam-Webster Dictionary*, s.v. "nostalgia," accessed April 8, 2025, https://www.merriam-webster.com/dictionary/nostalgia.

that nostalgic experience. Nostalgia can be such an incredible experience. But what about when it's not, and it produces shame?

Recently, I had the opportunity to preach at a church in Myrtle Beach for a dear friend of mine. If my wife can't travel with me on a ministry trip, I always bring someone with me for accountability (to stay proactive in preventing trust issues). After service that night, one of my best friends, Jason Williams, and I were looking for a place to grab a milkshake. It was late, and we were driving down the main strip on North Ocean Boulevard, and I felt like bursting into tears. As we passed some of the hotels, restaurants, clubs, and bars, I started experiencing some nostalgia, and waves of shame were flooding my heart. It was at that beach, during the whole summer of my senior year of high school, that I made some wrong decisions to drink and smoke weed. For a couple of minutes on that drive, I felt like a failure, a loser, a disappointment, an embarrassment, unqualified, a hypocrite, and so very ashamed.

> **GOD DOESN'T GIVE GRACE SO YOU CAN CONTINUE TO LIVE IN SIN. GOD GIVES GRACE TO SET YOU FREE FROM SIN!**

I went to Mars Hill University on a football scholarship in the fall of that same year. It was on a Sunday morning when the football coach had the whole team attend church together at the

Mars Hill Baptist Church. I loved God, but I definitely wasn't living right or making the right decisions. I wish I could tell you something about that Sunday morning service, but I can't. I can't tell you who the pastor was or what he preached. I can't even tell you what songs we sang. However, it was in the middle of that service, in the most mundane moment, looking up at the ceiling fan, that God got hold of my heart, and the Holy Spirit rocked my world in a good way. Whatever He did, and however He did it, I knew instantly that I wasn't where I was supposed to be and that I needed to change. I left that service, called my parents, and gave up my plans to play college ball, and the rest is history!

That same year, God radically changed my life! First John 1:9 (NLT) says, "But if we confess our sins to him, he is faithful and just to forgive us our sins and to cleanse us from all wickedness." So, I humbled myself before God, repented of my sins, and received His grace in my life. God doesn't give grace so you can continue to live in sin. God gives grace to set you free from sin! I made a change and turned from that lifestyle. So, if you haven't repented before God and asked Him to forgive you for whatever you have done, start there. *You'll never be able to move forward with God's purpose, and you'll never be able to gain His trust to receive His blessings, without first making things right with Him.* Trust me, it's worth it!

FAILURE IS AN EVENT, BUT IT IS NEVER A PERSON!

JUSTIN GRAHAM

Several years ago, I brought my wife and kids to Mars Hill to visit that church. I walked into that sanctuary, and I knew exactly where I was sitting that Sunday morning back in college. I went straight to that pew, sat down, looked up at those same ceiling fans, and just cried tears of gratitude because I no longer had to walk around in the shame of my past—all because of Jesus! So now, when I hear songs, see people, or visit places that produce nostalgia in my heart, I turn it into praise. I don't sit in my shame, but instead, I rejoice in my salvation in Jesus! Those songs take me back. Certain people take me back. Certain places take me back. However, I don't have to look back in shame. I can look back with gratitude and praise God for His loving kindness and amazing grace!

YOU'RE IN GOOD COMPANY

It would be easy to say that God could never use or trust Moses because he disqualified himself. In the same way, it would be easy to say that I disqualified myself, and I'm sure it would be just as easy for you to say the same. The enemy of your faith will use shame against you so that you will feel like a failure with no hope of redemption. Hell wants you to believe that God could never trust you again. Satan wants you to believe the lie that says you have no hope of a blessed future because of your past. The good news is that you're in good company. There are so many heroes of the faith from the Bible with a shameful past that many would label a failure, unqualified, and untrustworthy.

Noah was a drunk.

Abraham, Isaac, and Jacob were all liars.

Samson was a womanizer.

Rahab was a prostitute.

David committed adultery and had someone murdered.

Gideon and Elijah bowed to fear.

Jonah was disobedient and ran from God.

Peter denied even knowing Jesus.

The woman at the well was four times divorced and living in adultery.

Paul was an arrogant and religious leader who had Christians murdered.

Moses was a murderer.

In one of King David's low points, the Bible says in 1 Samuel 30:6 (KJV) that he "encouraged himself in the LORD." When all of hell, along with people and places in your life, tries to bring you down with shame and condemnation, you need to learn to encourage yourself in the Lord. There are still moments when the devil will try to convince me that I'm nothing but a hypocrite. Sometimes, you have to learn how to preach to yourself! You need to remind the devil, or anyone else who might be trying to discourage you, that they don't know you. They just knew the old you! No matter what you've done and no matter where you've been, there's still hope for you. And that hope is found in Jesus! No matter the setback, the embarrassment, or the trust that's been broken, there's hope for you! Failure is an event, but it is never a person! Every saint has a past, and every sinner has a future! You're in good company.

Turn every painful, nostalgic memory into praise and move forward. You cannot afford to stay stuck and sit in your shame. You will never fulfill your purpose that way, and that mindset will only increase your trust issues. Every memory of your past is a moment to praise God for His grace! *News flash: God does not allow you to look back on your past so you will live in guilt and shame. He allows you to look back so you are reminded of His grace and salvation!*

I can take you to some places, and I can tell you of some things that I'm not very proud of. But it's those places and those things that remind me of God's grace! It's taken me some time throughout the years to figure out how to get to where I am today. It was not instantaneous; rather, it was a process, but today, every time I think about the mistakes I've made, I tell the devil to shut up, and I give God praise for His grace!

It's the Friday nights at the club that remind me of grace!

It's the times that I smoked one too many and got high that remind me of grace!

It's the times that I looked at pornography that remind me of grace!

It's the times that I told God I wouldn't, but I did anyway that remind me of grace!

It's the times that I've said things way out of line that remind me of grace!

It's the times that I was a terrible, hypocritical so-called Christian that remind me of grace!

It's the times that I've made some wrong, untrustworthy decisions that remind me of grace!

If you're perfect, then you might as well just put this book down because it's not for you. But if you find yourself living with any regret, feeling like you don't deserve God's love, feeling like a failure, and unworthy of trust because of the mistakes of your past, you are in good company! *There is hope for you! Your past is simply a reminder of God's grace and His wonderful love for you!* He loves you deeply! In fact, there's nothing you could have done, and there's no place you could have gone that can, or ever will, take you away from His love!

> ## NEVER ALLOW SHAME TO PULL YOU BACK TO SIN. LEAN INTO GRACE SO YOU CAN GET CLOSER TO GOD.

There's a story of a father who had two sons in Luke chapter 15. The younger one hit a rebellious streak and told his dad that he wanted to move out. He was tired of living under his expectations. He asked his father to give him his share of the inheritance, which was a slap in his father's face. However, his father agreed and sent him on his way. That son made a huge mistake living wildly and recklessly. He blew through all the money and ended up broke and homeless, with no place to live and nothing to eat. The Bible tells us that when that son "came to his senses" (v. 17, NIV), he remembered his father's house. He said, "If I can just get back to my father's house, maybe he'll allow me to at least be one of his servants" (v. 19, author paraphrase). As he was on his way back, his father saw him in the distance, ran to meet him, and gave him the biggest hug ever. His dad said, "Bring him the best robe, put a ring on his finger, get him some shoes, and bring the fattened calf because we're about to celebrate! My lost son has come home!" (vv. 22-24, author paraphrase). There is no shame when you turn to God! There is only redemption. Just like the lost son, be reminded when you look back over your life of our loving God who will always welcome you back home no matter what you've done or where you've been!

When you look back . . . see the Cross of Jesus!
When you look back . . . see how God kept you!
When you look back . . . see how God has provided for you!
When you look back . . . see God's faithfulness!
When you look back . . . see how far you've come!
When you look back . . . see how much you have to be thankful for!
When you look back . . . discover that there is no more shame!

You may not be where you want to be with God yet. You may not be who you want to be in Christ yet. And you may feel like God could never trust you again. However, you need to take a moment and praise God that, at least, you're not where you used to be or who you used to be! Let's decide today to move forward!

CHARCOAL AND GRACE

In the first few years of The Avenue Church, there was a young man who gave his life to Christ and experienced a radical life change. He was addicted to drugs and a deadbeat dad, and in a miracle moment, when he surrendered his life to God, he dropped the drugs and became the dad his kids and his wife needed him to be for their family. A couple of years went by, and everything seemed to be going great. He approached me on a Sunday morning in late summer as the fall months were approaching.

He said, "Pastor, I'm embarrassed and feel stupid asking you to pray for me about something." I assured him that he could trust me, and he proceeded to tell me his concern. He said, "It's getting ready to turn fall, and I'm worried that I'm going to turn back to drugs." At first, I was super confused, but I continued to listen. He added, "This sounds so dumb, but everyone, including myself, wears hoodies in the fall. Every time I used to get high, I was always wearing hoodies. It reminds me of how I used to be, and I don't want to return back to my old ways."

I encouraged him to change the way he sees the memory of his past. I told him to turn it into praise because that is no longer who he is. I made sure he was surrounded with people for account-ability, and we prayed like crazy. Looking back produced nostalgic feelings that tempted him to go back to his old ways. He was sitting in that shame the enemy was throwing at him. At the end of the day, you have a choice to make: live free with God's grace or get stuck in sin and shame. Unfortunately, he chose to look back in shame and turned back to sin, and the jury is still out on whether he'll ever make a comeback. Never allow shame to pull you back to sin. Lean into grace so you can get closer to God.

It's all fun and games when nostalgia reminds you of the good times. But what about the nostalgia that produces shame and pulls you back into a sinful lifestyle? What about the painful reminders? What about memories that tempt you to quit? What do you do when you feel like you can never be trusted again?

In John chapters 18 and 21, we see this unfold right before our eyes. Jesus had been crucified, had risen from the dead, and had made His way around the region. When He showed up to the disciples, Peter, the leader of the pack and one of, if not the closest, to Jesus, struggled to even face Jesus. Peter had screwed up in a major way. The last interaction Peter had with Jesus was right before Jesus's arrest and crucifixion. It was a conversation that Peter would never forget. Jesus warned Peter that he would deny knowing Him the night before the crucifixion. Without hesitation, Peter was adamant that he would never do that. Well, Peter did the very thing he said he would never do and denied knowing Jesus . . . three times! The Bible tells us that he was standing around a charcoal campfire right outside where Jesus was being held as a prisoner when he denied Him. So, Jesus heard his chief apostle and friend deny that he knew Him. Could you imagine if the last words Jesus heard you say were that you never knew Him? Talk about shame!

After Jesus's death on the cross, and after He rose from the dead, Peter struggled because every time he saw Jesus, all he could think about was his failure. That mistake (times three) made him want to give up. So, Peter decided to go back to fishing because at least he was good at it. He had royally messed up. There was no way that Jesus would ever trust him again. While he was out fishing, Jesus called out to Peter from the shore. Peter was overwhelmed with emotion and took off running in the water to meet Jesus. Upon his arrival, Jesus was cooking some fish around a charcoal campfire! In a moment, nostalgia brings Peter right back to the night of his greatest failure when he denied Christ around a charcoal campfire! There are only two times in the entire New Testament that charcoal is even mentioned, and both times are with Peter. Jesus understands how hell will try to use shame against you, and He knew it would be an issue for Peter, so He decided to confront it head-on with grace.

At this lakefront cookout, Jesus gave Peter an opportunity for redemption. Three times, Jesus asked Peter if he loved Him. Peter answered back with a resounding "yes" all three times. Three times the redemption for the three times of regret. To get the full impact of this moment, we must go back to the original Greek language of the word "love" used in this passage. Jesus used the word *agapaō* (*agapē*) for love the first two times He asked Peter. *Agapē* is a selfless, sacrificial, and unconditional love.[14] It's used to describe the love of God for humanity. However, Peter responded with a different word. Peter used the word *phileō* for love. It describes a warm, tender, and personal love, marked for friendship and respect.[15] *Phileō* is one level under *agape*. Jesus saw Peter's transparency, brokenness, and honesty, so He decided to change the word on the third and final attempt. He asked, "Peter, do you *phileō* me?" Once again, Peter responded, "Yes Lord, I *phileō* you." In fact, we're told that this last time hurt Peter because he realized that his love for God could never match God's love for him. So, Jesus was letting Peter know that He understood he was only human and would make mistakes. Jesus was coming down to meet Peter where he was. He was saying, "I'll accept your love because all I want is your heart!"

14 *Logos Bible Software*, s.v. "agapē," accessed April 8, 2025, https://www.logos.com/.
15 *Logos Bible Software*, s.v. "phileō," accessed April 8, 2025, https://www.logos.com/.

YOUR SIN AND SHAME ARE NO MATCH FOR THE POWER OF GOD'S GRACE!

Jesus was showing Peter that he had to stop sitting in shame about his past, and the same applies to you. There's nothing you can do about your past, and there's nothing good for you in your past! You do not belong in your past. It's time to move forward into the purpose that God has for your life. No matter your past, no matter what you've done, and no matter where you've been, God's grace is greater! God will accept your *phileō* love because your heart is all He desires from you! Jesus used the charcoal to replace the memory of his failure with a new memory of His grace! Every time the enemy tries to throw your past in your face to shame you so that you'll return to your sin, turn it all into praise! Praise God that His love for you is, and will always be, unconditional. *Move forward by standing on God's Word and remind yourself that there's nothing good for you in taking the bait and returning to sin!*

Second Corinthians 5:17 (NKJV) says, "Therefore, if anyone *is* in Christ, *he is* a new creation; old things have passed away; behold, all things have become new." In other words, with Jesus, you're not the failure of your past. You're not the disappointment of your setbacks! In fact, your sin and shame are no match for the power of God's grace! God still wants to do great things in you, for you, and through you!

Shame on you? No! It's time to break the shame off you! The devil is a liar!

Romans 8:1 (NIV) says, "Therefore, there is now no condemnation for those who are in Christ Jesus." After Moses committed murder, he was still able to earn God's trust. God allowed him to lead millions of people out of bondage and into a covenant with Him. After Peter denied the Savior, he was still able to earn God's trust. God allowed him to lead thousands of people to Christ, which has had a ripple effect throughout history. Now, millions and millions of people have become followers of Christ. God still allows me to give it my all in earning His trust, even after making some of the dumbest mistakes of my life. When the enemy tries to throw shame in my face, I turn it into praise and thank God for His grace. So now, when I have to drive by the *Playboy* magazine house, I don't sit in my shame; I'm reminded of grace. Whenever I smell the charcoal in the park, in my neighborhood, or even in my own backyard, I just smile, thank God for His amazing grace, and rejoice in how He's given me another chance for redemption. My prayer for you as you read this book is that you will understand that God is for you and really does want to trust you!

If God could trust Moses to lead His people to the Promised Land after committing murder . . . you can still gain His trust!

If God could trust Peter to lead a movement that would change the world after he denied even knowing Him . . . you can still gain His trust!

If God could trust this pastor to lead a church to win thousands to Jesus . . . you can still gain His trust!

HERE'S THE BIG IDEA:

Rise up out of shame and start moving forward to earn God's trust. God's grace will help you eliminate your trust issues!

CONSIDER:

- What things or places of your past bring you shame?
- Do you allow shame to keep you from moving forward with God's purpose for your life?

CHALLENGE:

- Go get some charcoal this week and light it on fire in your grill at home or in a park, and spend a few moments just giving God praise for His grace.

PRAYER:

Heavenly Father,
Please forgive me for every sin that I have committed throughout
my life that has caused You to not trust me. Thank You for
Your amazing grace! I refuse to allow Satan to keep me stuck
in shame. I'm ready to move forward with Your purpose and
plan for my life. I give You praise because I am not who I
used to be, but I am who You say I am. Lord, because of You,
I have hope and I am redeemed! In Jesus's name. Amen!

CHAPTER 7

NOTHING ELSE MATTERS

WALMART AT 2 a.m. can cause you to question everything you know to be true in life. In the year we were in Cincinnati, Ohio, serving as youth pastors, both of our kids got sick at the same time with the flu. As young parents, we weren't yet experts at making sure the medicine cabinet was filled with the essentials for times like those. So, when both were running high fevers in the middle of the night, I headed to Walmart to get something that would help bring their fevers down. On the way to the store, I remember thinking, *I'm so thankful that there's a place open in the middle of the night for this.* I thought it would be a painless and quick trip where I could run in, grab the medicine, and head back home in just a few short minutes. I was wrong!

As I made my way through the front doors, I witnessed things that I wasn't prepared to see. People who I'm sure did not think twice about what they were wearing before they left their houses were shopping. Some of these individuals had kids with them—running around the store barefoot! Being the germaphobe that I am, I thought, *Where are their parents?* only to quickly realize that

I already knew that answer. Let's just say I saw things that night that shocked me and woke me up really quickly.

Trying to stay focused on my assignment, I went to the medicine aisle, grabbed what I needed, and headed to the checkout. I was on the home stretch until I turned the corner and found only one checkout lane open; the line was backed all the way up to one of the store aisles. (This was before the self-checkout lanes that I'm so thankful for today.) I counted almost fifteen carts, some pretty full of groceries. I took a deep breath and started calculating in my head how long this would probably take. Judging by the items and carts that I saw, I knew it was going to take at least forty-five minutes to get through that line. That's when I started to question some things about myself.

> **INTEGRITY IS THE UNWAVERING DETERMINATION IN THE HEART TO DO RIGHT, NO MATTER WHAT.**

Don't judge me, but I started contemplating something that I normally would never do. I thought, *This is one bottle of medicine. I could just walk out, and no one would ever know.* I was shocked I even had that thought, but my so-called sanctified mind had it. While I was rehearsing some really stupid scenarios, the Holy Spirit did what He does best—He simply thumped my heart and said, *Really, Justin? Wow!* I took a deep breath and, even though

I could have said it aloud and no one would have even noticed with the surrounding chaos, I internally answered Him back, *No, I'm not going to steal it!* One hour later, I walked out of Walmart with the medicine I purchased and with my integrity still intact!

Integrity is defined as a "firm adherence to a code of especially moral or artistic values; the quality or state of being complete or undivided."[16] When you take the time to study the Bible, integrity is clearly a heart issue. Integrity is the unwavering determination in the heart to do right, no matter what. It's doing the right thing, regardless of the outcome and no matter who it affects or how it affects them. Being a person of integrity is the secret to solving your trust issues. Billy Graham said:

> *[Integrity] means a person is the same on the inside as he or she claims to be on the outside. He is the same person alone in a hotel room a thousand miles from home as he is at work or in his community or with his family. A man of integrity can be trusted.*[17]

In other words, a person of integrity is the one God trusts.

INSTANT REGRET

In Numbers 20, we find Moses doing an amazing job following God's instructions and being an incredible leader for the Israelites. He had successfully gone into arguably one of the most powerful kingdoms and stood up to Pharaoh to lead them to freedom. He led them through one of the most amazing miracles of the Bible at the Red Sea. He was able to hear from God and

16 *Merriam-Webster Dictionary*, s.v. "integrity," accessed April 8, 2025, https://www.merriam-webster.com/dictionary/integrity.
17 Billy Graham, "[Integrity] means a person . . . can be trusted," *Billy Graham Library*, 13 Feb. 2021, https://billygrahamlibrary.org/blog-10-quotes-from-billy-graham-on-integrity/.

organized them into a strong army. Moses gained God's trust and was allowed to speak and hear directly from Him. God even used Moses to perform several miracles while out in the wilderness. Whenever the Israelites moaned and complained time and time again about the accommodations, food, and water, Moses met with God to work out a solution. Moses even convinced God a couple of times to change His mind about destroying the Israelites because of their complaining and disobedience to His commands. Moses had truly gained God's trust.

TRUST TAKES TIME TO ESTABLISH AND CAN BE UNDONE IN A SINGLE MOMENT.

Once again, the Israelites got impatient with Moses because they were struggling to find water. That wasn't the first time it had happened, so he took the situation to God, and Moses was instructed to speak to a rock so that water would pour out. One can only imagine how irritated Moses was with the Israelites at this point. The right thing would have been to do exactly what God told him to do, but that's not what Moses did. In his frustration, he raised his staff and hit the rock twice. Water did come out, but God was not pleased with Moses. God made a statement that screams at us from the page. The Lord said to Moses and Aaron in Numbers 20:12 (NIV), "Because you did not trust in me enough to honor me as holy in the sight of the Israelites, you will not bring this community into the land I give them."Talk about instant regret! Can you imagine the flood of emotions that had to have swept through Moses? He had worked extremely hard for so many years to gain God's trust, and one slip of integrity caused it all to unravel. After all they had been through, Moses wasn't allowed to enter the Promised Land because of one moment that resulted in trust issues!

Of all God's people, Moses was the one He trusted, and with one wrong move, it felt like he was back at square one. Trust takes time to establish and can be undone in a single moment. Do you think Moses would have hit the rock if he had known it would have caused trust issues and prevented him from entering the Promised Land? Absolutely not! God didn't allow Moses to enter the Promised Land because He was more concerned about his integrity. If Moses had known then what we know now, he wouldn't have hit the rock. If you had known that inappropriate text would ruin your marriage, would you still have sent it? If you had known that one drink would turn you into an alcoholic, would you still have taken the sip? If you had known that dishonesty would get you fired, would you still have lied about that situation? What good is the promise if you lose yourself and break trust in the process? Without integrity, there is no trust. You'll always regret making the wrong decisions, but you'll never regret making the right ones. You'll never regret becoming a person of integrity. *Without integrity, nothing else matters. Without integrity, God can't and won't trust you.* It matters how you live!

IT'S THE LITTLE THINGS

My wife loves to poke fun at me by calling me a rule follower. I can take it because it really is pretty funny. She laughs until she needs my help with things like putting a shelf back together that she miserably failed to assemble because she didn't want to follow the instructions. She laughs when I get so frustrated at the people who drive by the sign that says, "MERGE, LEFT LANE CLOSED AHEAD." Being the rule follower that I am, I merge, and I'll even let people get over in front of me until I know they've been warned for almost a mile but still try to get over at the last minute after they passed everyone else who followed the rule. At some point, I refuse to let anyone over. It will be a cold day in hell before I let them over! I will hit the car in front of me before I let them over! Why? Because I'm following the rules! My wife still laughs at me about it today because we debate about who's actually following the proper traffic laws in that situation. Either way, I feel justified!

Moses's actions, according to our standards, seem justifiable. What's the big deal about striking a rock? He was just as frustrated with the people as anyone would have been. It seems like such a small, meaningless issue—disobedience—but it's a big issue. When it comes to trust, it doesn't matter how big or small the issue is. If doing the right thing is important when it comes to something like murder, then doing the right thing is important with something like obeying God's instructions to speak to a rock. *When it comes to integrity, every decision is important!* How you live matters. Everything you say and don't say matters. Everything you do and don't do matters. However, way too many people live by their own standards rather than God's. In turn, people try to justify their actions even when they know they're wrong. We love the idea of being a trustworthy person of integrity, so we justify our actions to feel good about the wrong decisions we have made.

YOUR PUBLIC PERCEPTION IS DIRECTLY CONNECTED TO YOUR PRIVATE PRACTICES.

We live in a self-absorbed, self-consuming, and self-centered society. People will make decisions based primarily on how they will benefit from them. If you're going to be a person of integrity and gain God's trust and that of others, you're going to have to learn to make the right decisions, regardless of whom it will affect and how it will affect the outcome. Contractors and engineers refer to the integrity of steel. Two pieces of steel may both look great on the outside, with no apparent difference between them. However, one of them may not support the weight when it's put under stress because its integrity has been compromised. Meanwhile, the other piece of steel holds up under stress because it has integrity. Maybe the reason God is struggling to trust you is because you lack integrity, which is causing you to crumble under the pressures of life! *Integrity equals zero compromise!* The little things are just as important as the big things. Personally, the reason why I make a big deal over life's little integrity issues is because if I can't master the little things, I will fall on my face when given the big things.

Integrity is making the right decision in front of people when it's a big deal. It's also making the right decision when you're all alone, and it doesn't seem like a big deal. Who are you in private when no one else is watching? Who are you in public when everyone is watching? One of my mentors, Dr. David Horton said to me, "The measure of God's anointing in public is linked to how we worship in private." Your public perception is directly connected to your private practices. The same principle applies here as well. If who you are in public doesn't match who you are in private, then who you are in public is fake! *News flash: God cannot trust fake people!* The wrong decision in public is still the wrong decision in private, and doing the right thing in public is still the right thing in private.

TALK IS CHEAP WHEN THERE'S NO PROOF OF YOUR TESTIMONY.

Trust is built with integrity, and this world needs people who will refuse to compromise on God's Word! I'm so tired of witnessing hypocritical people try to impress others in public only to insult God in private! *Impressing people is not impressive to God.* If you want to impress God and earn His trust, then gain integrity! I can say this next part because I'm a pastor. This world has had enough celebrity preachers who can work up a shout and hype up a crowd at church but live like hell and lose honor at home! I want to live my life in such a way that God, my wife, my kids, my church, and our community can see that I am trustworthy! I'm not perfect, but if I can't practice what I preach, then I need to shut up and sit down because nothing else matters!

In Matthew 18:6 (NIV), Jesus said, "If anyone causes one of these little ones—those who believe in me—to stumble, it would be better for them to have a large millstone hung around their neck and to be drowned in the depths of the sea." If my decisions cause those who look up to me and trust me to stumble, then I need to do some repenting because how I live matters, and the same goes for you. Buckle up right here because I'm challenging you and calling you to a higher, godly standard of living. Talk is cheap when there's no proof of your testimony. Maybe others in your life (including God) have trust issues with you because they've witnessed how you live. Don't be the reason why someone sins or turns away from God, all because they saw you live a double-standard life. If you say you're a Christian, then live it 24/7! Work hard at being who you say you are because nothing else matters!

- Show up to your job on time and be the hardest worker there ... and stop stealing company time and money by goofing off on social media.
- Stay faithful to your spouse and choose love every day ... and stop hiding and deleting messages from that person you shouldn't be talking to anyway.
- Always be a loyal friend and take up for them when someone tries to start something behind their back.

- Don't have different expectations for your kids than you have for yourself. If it's wrong for them to cuss, stop cussing. If it's wrong for them to drink, stop drinking.
- Follow through with your commitments. If you say you're going to do something, then do it.
- Be the Christian in private that you say you are in public because nothing else matters!

Integrity is a choice, and so is eliminating trust issues. No one can make you sin. You have to be determined to disconnect from it so you can connect more with God. I do a combination of little things in my life to gain trust. For example, I have software on my phone, iPad, and computer that tracks everywhere I go online. If I go anywhere or view anything that's questionable, it sends it to my accountability partners, and the first one is my wife. I do this to ensure that I never take the bait and sever trust. Trust is built with integrity, and every time you maintain it, you gain God's trust and the trust of others. When you become a person of godly integrity, you're taking the limits off what God can do in you, for you, and through you! Integrity opens heaven up over your life, and you don't want to miss out on that! My prayer is that you will see that putting in the work to eliminate trust issues is worth heaven's blessings and favor.

CHECK YOUR CONNECTIONS

King David is another hero in the Bible who teaches us a lot about trust issues. As a young boy, he killed the Israelite's enemy, the Philistine giant named Goliath, with just a slingshot. When he became king, he was always ready for battle and never shied away from combat. But in 2 Samuel 11, we read a different narrative. Verse 1 says that when it was time for Israel to go off to war, "David remained in Jerusalem" (NIV) and refrained from the battle. He should have been out with the rest of the army, fighting with and for his nation. Instead, he completely isolated himself without the proper accountability that would protect him and keep him out of trouble. Isolation is one of integrity's enemies. If you're going to be a person of integrity, then you must surround yourself with the right people. *You will never be able to maintain integrity without accountability.* David removed himself from where he should have been, and that allowed the enemy of his faith an opportunity to bring destruction to his life.

One day, while walking on the roof of his palace, David noticed a beautiful woman named Bathsheba bathing nearby. He sent someone to find out who she was and then had a messenger bring her to him so he could have sex with her. What? This is the man of God, King David! This is the one that the Bible describes as "a man after God's own heart!" (1 Samuel 13:14). The problem is so easy to pinpoint: if David had been out fighting with his men, then he wouldn't have been in that compromising situation. But I believe it's just as important, if not more, to note that he didn't get Bathsheba all by himself. He talked to some random person about who she was and then had some messenger get her for him. In other words, David didn't get into that compromising situation all by himself. The right person would have declined David's request to get Bathsheba. If you want to be a person of integrity, you must connect yourself to the right men or women of God who will hold you accountable.

> # WHO AND WHAT YOU CONNECT TO WILL EITHER MAKE YOU OR BREAK YOU.

Without the proper connections, you'll never be able to maintain your integrity. It's easier to make wrong decisions when you isolate yourself from the right people. It's harder to sin and easier to be a trustworthy person of integrity when you surround yourself with accountability. The right connections will help keep you away from any and every sin that would compromise your integrity. First Corinthians 15:33 (NIV) says, "Bad company corrupts good character." This verse highlights why I strongly encourage you to get in and/or stay in church because you will become who you are around. It's easier to maintain your integrity when you're connected to the place where the power and the presence of God show up. It's hard to make wrong decisions when you're connected to the place of God, the presence of God, the Word of God, and the people of God. Who and what you connect to will either make you or break you, so get connected to a local church.

You need some people in your life who love you enough to:

. . . call you out when you're making dumb decisions!

. . . let you know when your attitude is pathetic!

. . . hold you accountable when you're tempted to sin!

. . . pray with you when you're struggling to maintain integrity!

. . . tell you the truth when all you really want to hear is something that will justify your sin!

. . . correct you so you can keep your connection with God!

David royally messed things up—he got Bathsheba pregnant while her husband, Uriah, was out fighting with Israel's army. Instead of coming clean with what they had done, David worked hard to justify his actions and cover it up when he brought Uriah home to have sex with his wife. It backfired on David because Uriah was a man of integrity and refused to spend time with Bathsheba because he knew he needed to be out fighting with the men. So, David put him on the front line of battle, where he knew Uriah would probably be killed. Uriah died in the war, and David hoped they were in the clear. That's when God sent the prophet Nathan to call David out for his sin and lack of integrity. David ended up repenting, and God forgave him and spared his life, but he still had to deal with the consequences of some crazy family issues. God will bring correction to you so that He can keep His connection with you.

Neither David nor Moses tried to justify their actions. They knew they were in the wrong and had compromised their integrity. They submitted themselves to God's sovereignty and continued to put their trust in Him. Likewise, we need to be grateful for the times God corrects us. What if God had not held them accountable? What could have happened to David and Moses? What I'd like to ask David and Moses is, "Was it worth it? Was striking the rock worth missing out on the Promised Land? Was disobeying God worth it? Was the one-night stand with Bathsheba worth it? Was all the family drama worth it?" I wholeheartedly believe the answer is a resounding, "No!" In fact, in Mark 8:36 (NLT), Jesus said it best: "What do you benefit if you gain the whole world but lose your own soul?" In other words, *what good is it to enjoy a moment of temporary satisfaction but compromise your integrity and eternity?*

I ask you the same question: Is the thing that's compromising your integrity worth it? What good is it if you're able to climb the corporate ladder of success but have to compromise your integrity to get there? What good is it if you're able to convince the whole world that you're the greatest person ever, but behind closed doors, you're a reckless nightmare? What good is it if you have public or online respect because of your platform but have lost all honor at home because of your irresponsible behavior? It's not worth it! Heaven is so much more important than the Promised Land for Moses and the public image for David, and that's why God didn't let their mistakes slide. It's the same reason why He won't let your compromise slide, either. He loves you too much! Nothing else but integrity matters. So, check your connections and embrace godly correction.

WHATEVER YOUR HEART DESIRES

Moses only had to disobey God once to miss out on the Promised Land, which seems really harsh. So, this whole integrity and trust issue thing may feel like an uphill climb and maybe an impossible expectation, but I promise you that you can do it. Remember Luke 12:48 (NLT) to keep things in perspective: "When someone has been given much, much will be required in return; and when someone has been entrusted with much, even more will be required." We're talking about Moses. This is someone with a very long history with God, and he knew better. I'm not trying to insult you, but I don't think you and I are on a Moses level yet. And I'm definitely not saying you have the green light to sin because you're not held to as high a standard as Moses. Sin is sin, right is right, and wrong is wrong. I'm simply saying that before you start worrying about how you would handle leading millions of people into an already occupied land, let's start with where you are. Let's start with getting our hearts in the right place with God. Start with being a person of your word and following through on your commitments. Start with being consistent and trustworthy with the seemingly little things and work your way up. *Trust is a heart issue,* and if you're going to be a person of integrity, that's where you need to start.

When I had the radical encounter with God at Mars Hill University that Sunday morning in church, I was so excited and, at the same time, completely overwhelmed because I had no idea what I was supposed to do or where to start. Psalm 37:4 (ESV) says, "Delight yourself in the LORD, and he will give you the desires of your heart." That doesn't mean that if you give your all to God, He'll give you whatever you want. It means that if you go all in with God, He will give your heart the right desires. In other words, the right delight will produce the right desire. So, that's exactly what I decided to do. I made a vow to the Lord that I didn't share with a soul. I told the Lord that I would give up every sport for an entire year because I had made that a god in my life—before that moment, sports were definitely more important to me than God. I decided to not even step on a court or a field for an entire year. I was determined to follow God and find out what He wanted for my life. Let's just say I was set on fire for Jesus, and it was awesome!

> ## THE RIGHT DELIGHT WILL PRODUCE THE RIGHT DESIRES.

I've never wanted to be a singer or a musician, but something so weird started happening to me. As I delighted myself in the Lord, I desired to be in a choir. I know you're thinking, *Okay, that's strange and random,* and I totally agree. The more on fire I became for Jesus, the more I wanted to be in a choir. I didn't know what to do with this weird desire, so I talked to Russ Arrigo, the youth pastor at my home church at that time. After what felt like a very awkward conversation because I didn't know how to explain things, he said, "Lee University has several choirs, and that's where your best friend, Adam Noe, is going." Honestly, I had never even thought about it, but in a moment, it was like a Times Square billboard lit up in my spirit, flashing "Go to Lee!"

Long story short, I transferred to Lee University solely to join the Lee University Campus Choir! And the rest is history. We traveled the world leading worship in countless churches. Our choir director, Dr. David Horton, mentored me. I met my beautiful best friend and bride in that choir. I discovered the call of God on my life in that choir. I met Brandon Ledford, who is now our worship pastor at The Avenue in that choir. One of the reasons I was hired as a youth pastor was because of my experience in that choir. And now, Adam and his wife, Jessica, Brandon and his wife, Amy, and Melissa and I get to be in ministry together because of what God did in our lives in that choir! My precious kids, Jocelyn and Judah, would not be here today if I had not joined that choir, and so much of The Avenue's culture is a result of what God did in my life in that choir! As I delighted myself in God, He gave me a desire that would lead me to my destiny!

Are you delighting in the right thing? Your desire is connected to your delight. The right delight will produce the right desires. Is your heart in the wrong place because of wrong desires? God was able to place in me the right desires that would lead me to my purpose and calling only when I got my heart in the right place. It all starts with the heart! Likewise, if your heart is not in the right place, you will never desire to be a person of integrity. If your heart is not in the right place, God will never be able to trust you. But, if you can get your heart in the right place and allow God to set it on fire for Him, your trust issues will be eliminated, and nothing else will matter. Trust me when I say that you want this! Trust and integrity are about to open up a new world to you that will blow your mind, and your whole life will never look or be the same!

HERE'S THE BIG IDEA:

Don't compromise your integrity for anyone or anything. It's not worth it! The secret places of your life are what need the most attention. The more you maintain your integrity, the more trust you earn!

CONSIDER:

- In what areas of your life are you compromising God's Word?
- Are the decisions you make in public and private consistent?
- Do you have a secret sin that's compromising your integrity?
- Do you have real friends who will hold you accountable and speak truth to you?
- Would you trust you?

CHALLENGE:

- Start spending some quality time with God daily by putting on some worship music while you read the Bible and pray.
- Reach out to someone you trust today and ask them to hold you accountable in the areas where you lack integrity.

PRAYER:

Heavenly Father,

Thank You for never giving up on me. Thank You for Your mercy that is new every day. Please forgive me for all the times I did what I said I would never do. Forgive me for dismissing sin in my life. Will you give me the strength to make daily decisions that honor You and are in line with Your Word? Surround me with the right people who I can trust to care enough about me to speak truth into my life. Set my heart on fire for You, Lord! Stir up inside of me a renewed passion for Your Presence and Your Word. My desire is to live with integrity and be someone You and everyone else in my life can trust. I give You full access to my heart. Show me the areas that I need to work on so I can eliminate any trust issues You may have with me. In Jesus's name. Amen!

CHAPTER 8

STOP CIRCLING THE MOUNTAIN

WE LIVE AT the foothills of the Great Smoky Mountains in East Tennessee, and it is arguably the most beautiful place on earth. I can look out and see the mountains every single day, and it still takes my breath away. Hiking is obviously very popular in this region, and I have always wanted to climb Mt. Le Conte. It has an elevation of 6,593 feet with a roundtrip hike of approximately thirteen miles (depending on the trail you take). I have said countless times throughout my life that I would climb that mountain one day, but I always had excuses to talk myself out of it. I have driven to Pigeon Forge and Gatlinburg a bazillion times, which sits at the base of Mt. Le Conte. I can be at one of the trails in less than an hour. I have circled that mountain my whole life and have never climbed it. That all changed in 2016 when several of the guys I was connected to at church decided to stop talking about it and finally make the climb.

Whenever you decide to climb a mountain, you don't just wake up one day and do it. You have to plan. You'll need to be in somewhat decent shape, and your knees and feet will have to be able to take the punishment you're about to put them through. You'll need the proper clothing, a backpack with water and snacks, and any emergency supplies that could help you if something were to go wrong. It's also really smart to go with others just in case you get hurt or find yourself in a dangerous situation. So, after some preparations and planning, we set out on that Saturday morning to climb Mt. Le Conte. It was time to stop circling that mountain and finally climb to the top to get a view of what I've always wanted to experience.

> **CONFESSION AND REPENTANCE GIVE YOU ACCESS TO GOD'S GRACE AND FORGIVENESS. FAITHFULNESS AND INTEGRITY GRANT YOU ACCESS TO GOD'S BLESSINGS AND TRUST.**

As we set out on our hike, I thought, *This is going to be a piece of cake because I'm a runner and try to stay in pretty good shape.* As soon as we got started, I knew I was in for a challenge because of how fast some of the guys wanted to go, combined with the elevation change. The further we got, the more wisdom kicked in, and we decided to change the pace so we didn't burn out before we got to the top. When we got halfway up, some of the guys started feeling the burn in their legs and knees. We stopped several times to rest, hydrate, and refuel with some calories.

At one point, one of the guys thought he would have to turn back because his knee was bothering him. We decided to push through so we could all make the summit together. The closer we got to the top, the faster I walked because I was so excited to finally experience the views across the peaks of the Smoky Mountains. Let's just say that it did not disappoint. We stayed at the top for a couple of hours because it was absolutely breathtaking to look out and take in the beauty of God's creation. The climb cost us, but it was definitely worth it!

BECOME A PROFESSIONAL BOXER

Blessings, breakthroughs, and miracles are waiting for you to deal with your trust issues. Trust me when I tell you that you want to become a trustworthy person. If you're ever going to be a person of integrity and gain God's trust and the trust of others, it will cost you.

When God made it known in Numbers 12:7 that Moses was the one He trusted, it wasn't because Moses had a really cool name, and it for sure wasn't because Moses woke up one day and decided he deserved to be tapped as Israel's leader. Let me remind you that Moses was a murderer on the run for forty-plus years before he ever earned God's trust and the trust of millions of other people. This shows us that confession doesn't equal trust. Confession and repentance give you access to God's grace and forgiveness. Faithfulness and integrity grant you access to God's blessings and trust. Moses faithfully served as a shepherd for forty years on the "backside of the wilderness" (Exodus 3:1, KJV) to prove his trustworthiness. The good news is that no matter what you've done, there's a pathway to earn trust or gain it back. Either way, it's going to take some time and work to become trustworthy.

If this feels like an uphill battle, that's because it is. If it all feels really hard, that's because it is, and that's why not everyone will make the climb to the top to receive the prize. Too many people will live their whole lives circling a mountain that they really want to climb. Don't be that person! Do something today about your trust issues so you can experience all that God has for your life. Take note of the apostle Paul's playbook in 1 Corinthians chapter 9. In verse 27 (NLT), he says, "I discipline my body like an athlete, training it to do what it should. Otherwise, I fear that after preaching to others, I myself might be disqualified." *You can earn trust only if you learn to embrace discipline.* The word "discipline" here in Greek is *hypōpiazō*.[18] It means "to strike a blow, to hit under the eye." Paul is using a boxing term to illustrate what it's going to take to experience the blessings that God has available for us. When boxers train, they allow their trainers to punch them in the stomach repeatedly so that they can learn how to take a hit. That's *hypōpiazō*! Paul uses such an intense word to emphasize how you need to be disciplined enough to do whatever it takes to achieve the reward. Gaining trust is an uphill battle, but it's worth it. Living with integrity is really hard, but it's worth it. Climbing that mountain is rough, but it's worth it! Blessings are waiting for you at the top!

18 *Logos Bible Software*, s.v. "hypōpiazō" accessed April 29, 2025, https://www.logos.com/.

> **TRUST IS EARNED BY CHOOSING INTEGRITY CONSISTENTLY INSTEAD OF OCCASIONALLY.**

In 1 Timothy 4:7-8 (NIV), Paul writes to his spiritual son, instructing him to:

> *Have nothing to do with godless myths and old wives' tales; rather, train yourself to be godly. For physical training is of some value, but godliness has value for all things, holding promise for both the present life and the life to come.*

The word "train" here in Greek is gymnazō. It means "to exercise and workout ... naked!"[19] Let's go! ... What kind of book is this?

Back in the day, athletes would train naked so nothing would get in their way or slow them down. In the same way, gaining trust will require you to eliminate anything that would slow you down or hold you back. What's holding you back? What sin have you allowed in your life that doesn't belong? If you want to earn trust, then you must get disciplined and train so you can climb that mountain. Your disciplines will determine who you will become and what you will accomplish, and I don't want you to miss out on what God wants to do in your life simply because you lacked discipline! Trust is earned by choosing integrity consistently instead of occasionally. It takes intentional effort to gain integrity and unlock God's blessings over your life. Eliminate

---

19 *Logos Bible Software*, s.v. "gymnazō" accessed April 29, 2025, https://www.logos.com/.

trust issues through discipline to take the limits off what God can do in your life.

YOU'RE GONNA PAY FOR THAT

For most things, you will pay whatever it costs for something you consider valuable. You will spend crazy amounts on things you consider important. For example, coffee drinkers in America will spend, on average, $1,500 a year for their favorite beverage. Why? Because it's valuable to them. Personally, I appreciate a solid shoe game. I have a fair share of shoes that I keep in good condition, so they'll last me a long time, and I have invested a lot in them because I consider them valuable. (I never want a coffee drinker to give me a hard time about my shoe game ever again!) We can argue the value of something all day long. We're willing to pay high dollars for anything we truly value.

> ## SOME PURCHASES ARE NOT WORTH THE PRICE YOU PAID!

At The Avenue Church, we like to provide good merch for people. We have shirts, hoodies, jackets, hats, notebooks, books, Bibles, etc. for people to purchase. We never profit from those items (in fact, most of the time, we barely break even) because making money is not our goal. We just enjoy providing people a way to represent their love for God with quality merch. Some items cost more than others, depending on the material and the design. One of our staff members tried to purchase some designs from Temu in hopes it would be a cheaper option for people. When the shirts came in, they did look pretty cool! However, when I went to try one on in my size, I felt like Chris Farley singing, "Fat guy in a little coat!"[20] It was hilarious because I could barely get the shirt on, and it fit me like spandex. I walked around the office for a few minutes in my extremely "skinny" style shirt just to get a few laughs. Some purchases are just not worth the price you pay, even when they seem like a good deal.

In 2 Samuel chapter 24, David was coming to the end of his reign as the King of Israel and nearing the end of his life. Throughout his life, he had seen some incredible things. He witnessed some amazing highs and some horrific lows. He had been a successful king, and God even labeled him "a man after God's own heart." He was thinking back over his life, the strength of the nation, and the size of his army, and the strength of the nation intrigued him. The Bible says in verse 1 (NIV) that "the anger of the LORD burned against Israel, and he incited David against them, saying, 'Go and take a census of Israel and Judah.'" But that doesn't accurately describe what actually happened.

First Chronicles 21:1 (NIV) more clearly explains why God was angry with David: "Satan rose up against Israel and incited David to take a census of Israel." In other words, David took the bait and allowed pride to creep into his heart and began to think, *Look at all I've accomplished! Let's see how great we really are!* He

---

20 Peter Segal, quote from *Tommy Boy* (March 31, 1995; Los Angeles, CA: Paramount Pictures).

counted 1.3 million able fighting men ready for battle! However, David quickly realized what a dangerous decision he had made. By the time we get to 2 Samuel 24:10, we learn that "David was conscience-stricken after he had counted the fighting men, and he said to the LORD, 'I have sinned greatly in what I have done. Now, LORD, I beg you, take away the guilt of your servant. I have done a very foolish thing.'" In a split second, David learned a hard lesson. Some purchases are not worth the price you paid! So, be careful with your purchases.

> **A LACK OF INTEGRITY WILL PRODUCE A LIFE OF DESTRUCTION.**

Can you imagine everything that possibly ran through David's mind? David did not forget his mistake with Bathsheba in 2 Samuel 11. He remembered the pain that particular sin caused him and his family. He remembered the consequences of those actions. He realized that God was trusting him to lead His people with integrity, so conviction from his mistake gripped him. He definitely didn't want to experience the repercussions of the things that sin births.

A lack of integrity will produce a life of destruction. David knew how serious this was because he remembered and was even there when Uzzah touched the ark of the covenant in 2 Samuel 6, disrespecting and dishonoring God's presence. The ark was where the presence of God resided in the Old Testament. David had an animal pull the ark into Jerusalem on a new cart when the priests were supposed to carry it on their shoulders. They were allowed to touch the poles but not the ark. So, when the ark hit a bump and started falling off the cart, Uzzah reached out to steady it. As a result of their disobedience, Uzzah died right before David's eyes. When the Bible says that David was "conscience-stricken," it's because he was convicted, and he remembered how valuable God's presence was in his life.

Many theologians believe that David wrote Psalm 24 during the time when Uzzah died. Verses 3-4 (NIV) say, "Who may ascend the mountain of the LORD? Who may stand in his holy place? The one who has clean hands and a pure heart." When David said, "Ascend the mountain of the Lord," he was referring to the location where the ark of the covenant was placed on the hill of Jerusalem. David was addressing the Levites, who were responsible for the House of God. He witnessed Uzzah die. So, to take the ark of the covenant to its place in the temple of God, they had to arrive at a place of purity in their lives. In other words, if you want to ascend the mountain of God to experience His blessings, then you need to get your heart and life right with Him. *Ascending the mountain of God is a call to trustworthiness!* It's a call to holiness. It's a call to integrity. It's a call to right living according to God's Word. It's a call to get rid of any sin in your life that is holding you back from experiencing all that God has for you. It will cost you, but it's totally worth it!

GET A DIVORCE

The word "ascend" in Hebrew is *ālâ*. It means "to climb, to cause to rise, to go up."[21] Hold onto that word for just a minute. Who, then, can ascend? If you want to rise up and experience the fullness of God in your life, if you want to go to another level in your life with God, if you want to experience everything that He has for you, and if you want to earn trust, then you need to have *clean hands* and a *pure heart*. Let's talk about clean hands first. The word "clean" here in Hebrew is *nāqî*. It means "blameless, free from evil or guilt, free from someone or something . . . unmarried."[22] Unmarried?

> **IF YOU'RE GOING TO BECOME TRUSTWORTHY TO ASCEND THE MOUNTAIN OF THE LORD, THEN YOU'RE GOING TO HAVE TO DIVORCE SIN AND GET BACK TO YOUR RESPONSIBILITY!**

Back then, a newlywed was relieved from his duty of going to war for an entire year. "Married" hands mean that you're not obligated to show up for battle. "Married" hands mean that you're able to go out and do your own thing. On the flip side, "unmarried" hands mean that you have a responsibility to maintain.

21 *Logos Bible Software*, s.v. "ālâ" accessed April 29, 2025, https://www.logos.com/.
22 *Logos Bible Software*, s.v. "nāqî" accessed April 29, 2025, https://www.logos.com/.

"Unmarried" hands mean that you can't check out and just do whatever you want. The problem is you may have gotten married but just to the wrong thing. Your sin and lack of integrity have broken God's trust in you, and you've neglected your responsibilities as a Christian. You've "married" sin, yet you think you still have access to God like you did when you were "unmarried" with clean hands! In other words, "unmarried clean hands" means you're not in covenant with sin—you're in covenant with God!

As a pastor, you probably won't hear me encourage many people to divorce, but in this chapter . . . I am! *News flash: If you're going to become trustworthy to ascend the mountain of the Lord, then you're going to have to divorce sin and get back to your responsibility!* It's time to get a DIVORCE! You need to divorce any and every sin in your life so you can finally stop circling the mountain that you really want to climb! You need to divorce that sin so you can eliminate the trust issues. You need to divorce that sin so you can ascend the mountain of the Lord. You may realize right now that you have purchased something that was not worth the price you paid. You may even realize that you have married something that's holding you back from ascending and going higher with the Lord. It's time to shake yourself free from that dead weight that's keeping you stuck at the base of the mountain! You need freedom from sin today! You need a divorce!

Divorce . . . *the addiction!*
the pornography!
the hypocrisy!
the spiritual impurity!
the lies!

the bitterness!
the pride!
the gluttony!!
the self-entitlement!
the lukewarmness!

> **IF YOUR HEART IS NOT IN THE RIGHT PLACE, THEN YOUR HANDS WILL REVEAL YOUR SECRETS.**

You need to divorce that sin so you can get back to your responsibilities and go higher with God! It's so much better to ascend the mountain of the Lord, where you can experience God's presence and His blessings, than to remain stuck and miserable in sin at the base.

Let's return to our scripture in Psalm 24. "Who can ascend the mountain of the Lord? He who has clean hands and a *pure heart.*" The word "pure"" here in Hebrew is *bǎr.* It means "empty, having no faults, sincere."[23] In Matthew 5:8 (NIV), Jesus said, "Blessed are the pure in heart, for they will see God." Having a pure heart will cost you, but it is worth it. Having a pure heart is all about having the right motives. If you're ever going to have clean hands, then you need to have right motives first. If your heart is not in the right place, then your hands will reveal your secrets. In other

---

23 *Logos Bible Software*, s.v. "bǎr" accessed April 29, 2025, https://www.logos.com/.

words, your actions will tell on your heart! You'll have to stop making impulsive purchases that you know you'll regret in order to ascend. When you pay for sin, you will regret your purchase. Sin is so easily accessible because it's cheap and worthless, but never forget that you get what you pay for!

> **REMAINING AT A LOW ALTITUDE IS NO WAY TO LIVE WHEN GOD HAS CREATED YOU TO ASCEND AND GO HIGHER!**

In 2 Samuel 24, David remembered that some purchases are not worth the price you pay. He has come face to face with his own words, "Who can ascend the hill of the Lord?" He was coming to the end of his life and remembering how bad it was to feel like God's presence had left him. He was remembering how terrible it was to break God's trust in him. He was remembering how awful he felt when he was living a double life and in sin with Bathsheba. So, David immediately repented for what He had done. Personally, I can tell you of some times, and I can take you to some places, that remind me of what it feels like to be at the bottom without God. I refuse to go back to that life! My prayer is that you will join me and do the same. If you're going to go to the next level with God, then you will need to work on the secret place of your life. It's a heart issue!

God is looking for people He can trust to live with integrity. He's looking for some pastors, leaders, moms, dads, young people, students, and churches that He can trust. He's looking for people who will have clean hands and pure hearts. Remaining at a low altitude is no way to live when God has created you to ascend and go higher! It's time to refuse to settle for less than what God has for you. Remember how bad things were in the mess you were in, and refuse to go back to that lifestyle. Remember how empty that sin left you. Remember how defeated you felt. Remember feeling far from God. Start fresh today by making up your mind to do whatever it takes to get clean hands and a pure heart so you can ascend to the Lord to receive His blessings and favor!

THE VIEW IS PRICELESS

When Melissa and I were youth pastors, we visited Dream City Church a few times in Phoenix, Arizona, for a pastor's conference. I'm grateful that this church welcomed us to learn and equipped us with tools for ministry. One unique quality of the church is that it sits at the bottom of a small mountain. They call it their "prayer mountain" and encourage people to climb it to spend some time at the top in prayer and worship. I took them up on that offer and climbed it several times throughout the years. One year, Melissa decided to join me on the hike. As we set out for the walk, I let her lead the way and set the pace. I told her to take her time because of the steep climb that resulted in a quick altitude shift. She gave me a "Yeah, yeah," and off she went. It wasn't too long into the ascent that she started breathing pretty hard and said, "I need to take . . ." and that's all she got out. She passed out right in front of me! Thankfully, I was able to stop her fall and sit her up to rest against the side of a rock. Let's just say it was a classic "I told ya so" moment. We ended up making it all the way to the top, and the view was stunning! Ascending the mountain cost Melissa something. She passed out, but it was definitely worth the climb to worship and pray together at the top of that mountain.

> **PEOPLE WHO DON'T KNOW THE VALUE OF THE PRESENCE OF GOD ARE SATISFIED WITH A LIFE OF DEFEAT THAT CHEAP SIN CAUSES!**

After David repented for what he had done with the army census, he needed to build an altar and make a sacrifice to God to make things right with Him. So, he went to a man named Araunah and asked if he could purchase his threshing floor to build the altar. Once Araunah found out what it was for, he offered it to David for free, along with the animals for the sacrifice. However, David said, "No, I insist on paying you for it. I will not sacrifice to the LORD my God burnt offerings that cost me nothing" (2 Samuel 24:24, NIV). Earlier, I told you to remember the Hebrew word for "ascend" (*ālâ*) because it connects to this scripture. The word "sacrifice" here in Hebrew is also *ālâ*.[24] It's

---

24 *Logos Bible Software*, s.v. "ālâ," accessed April 29, 2025, https://www.logos.com/.

the same word! It means "to ascend, to climb, to go up." David said, "I will not sacrifice (ascend) to the Lord my God with burnt offerings that cost me nothing." Matthew Henry said this about this scripture: "Those know not what religion is whose chief care it is to make it cheap and easy to themselves, and who are best pleased with that which costs them least pains or money. What have we our substance for but to honour God with it?"[25] In other words, people who don't know the value of the presence of God are satisfied with a life of defeat that cheap sin causes!

After David makes this sacrifice, he says in 1 Chronicles 22:1 (NIV) that "the house of the LORD God is to be here, and also the altar of burnt offering for Israel." The threshing floor that David purchased from Araunah is the exact site where the temple of God was built! The temple was built on a piece of property that cost David greatly!

Ascending should cost us something because it's at the top that we get to experience the best of God! David offered up worship, and it cost him something.

> **ANYONE CAN SIN BECAUSE IT'S CHEAP. BUT NOT EVERYONE WILL LIVE RIGHT BECAUSE IT'S EXPENSIVE!**

25 Matthew Henry, "Those who know . . . honour God with it?", *Bible Gateway: Matthew Henry's Commentary*, https://www.biblegateway.com/resources/matthew-henry/2Sam.24.18-2Sam.24.25.

David paid a big price for that spot because he desperately needed the presence of God to show up in his life and understood its value! If you're going to ascend, it will cost you. To ascend, you must say "no" to sin and "yes" to integrity! Every time you say "yes" to sin, you say "no" to God's blessings and cause trust issues! On the other hand, every time you say "no" to sin, you say "yes" to God's blessings and gain God's trust! Anyone can sin because it's cheap. But not everyone will live right because it's expensive!

Ascending is expensive. David knew that if he was going to survive, move forward with God, and get back to having clean hands and a pure heart, he had to make a sacrifice. *A faith that doesn't cost you anything is worth nothing, so if ascending doesn't cost you something, then it's not worth anything!*

Ascending is living by faith and not by feeling!

It's making the hard decisions when compromise is easier!

It's living with integrity so God will trust you!

It doesn't cheapen God's presence!

It's saying, "I would rather have Jesus than any sin!"

It's saying, "I would rather have Jesus than any drug, addiction, pride, arrogance, selfishness, or bitterness!"

It's saying, "I would rather have Jesus than live a hypocritical life!"

Ascending is about calling you to a higher standard of living without apologizing for righteousness. It's time to stop circling the mountain that will change your entire life! Stop saying, "One day, I will," and let that day be today! You need to learn the value of ascending because the experience at the top is worth the climb and the cost. The presence of God is worth the cost!

God's favor on your life is worth the climb! God's blessings are worth the ascension! Life at the top is where you want to live because that's the place where God's power shows up. It's that power that saves, heals, redeems, sets free, strengthens, restores, and breaks the stronghold of depression, fear, and anxiety! Life at the top changes everything for all eternity. *Stop circling and start climbing!*

When you see the temple mount in Jerusalem, you see what it cost somebody. We see the same thing with Jesus. The only way to be made right with God and have clean hands and a pure heart is through the blood of Jesus that was shed on the cross. So, when you see the cross, you're seeing what your salvation cost somebody. You cost God His only Son, but you are worth it! The climb to the top will cost you, but it's worth the ascent. Earning God's trust will cost you, but it's worth the ascent. Your purpose is worth it! Your calling is worth it! Your family is worth it! Your children are worth it! Your marriage is worth it! Your future is worth it! Ascending will cost you, but it's forever worth it! When you do your part in the natural, God will show up with the supernatural in your life. When God sees you working hard to be the one He can trust, He will respond and meet you with blessings and favor that will change your life. Go up! It's worth it!

HERE'S THE BIG IDEA:

If you'll pay the price to earn God's trust, He will allow you to ascend to another level where He will pour out His blessings and favor on your life! You're going to pay for the climb, but it's worth every penny!

CONSIDER:

- Where in your life are you lacking discipline that keeps you circling the mountain?
- What's holding you back from being trustworthy?
- What sin do you need to divorce?
- What is one thing that would have the biggest impact on your life if you were to stop doing it today?
- What is one thing that would have the biggest impact on your life if you were to start doing it today?
- Are you willing to pay the price to ascend the mountain of the Lord?

CHALLENGE:

- Be intentional and schedule time daily to worship God, pray, and read the Bible.
- If you're physically able, get some people together to go on a walk or a hike. At some point during the walk, tell them about what you're reading and share how you're tired of circling the mountain. Share what you've committed to leaving behind that will free you to ascend to the top where you can experience all that God has for your life. Tell them that you're working on eliminating your trust issues, and invite them to join you in your journey.

PRAYER:

Heavenly Father,
You are wonderful, and I am so grateful for Your love. I repent for
participating in sin and allowing things in my life that don't belong
because they dishonor You. Please forgive me! Create in me a pure
heart, and renew a right spirit within me, so that I can learn to
live with clean hands. Help me to hide Your Word in my heart so
that I will not sin against you. Earning Your trust is priceless to
me. I desire to be pleasing to Your heart more than I want to receive
any blessing from Your hand. Please give me the strength to be
disciplined enough to ascend Your mountain. In Jesus's name. Amen!

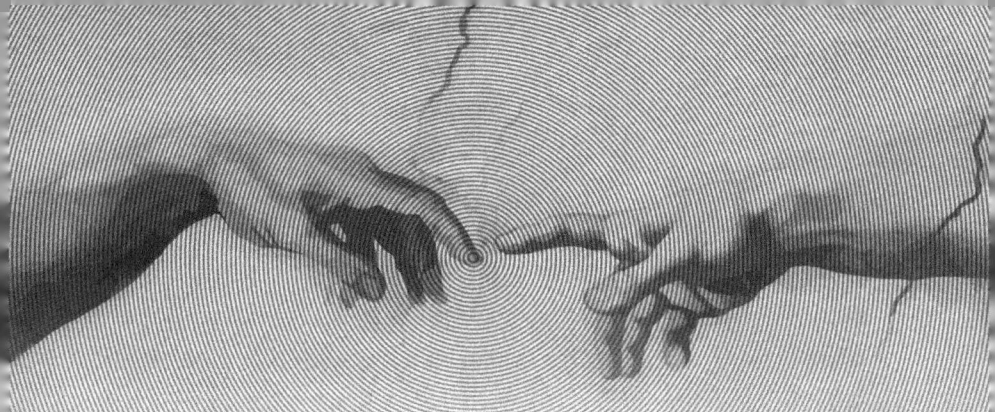

CHAPTER 9

GOD TRUSTS SERVANT LEADERS

THE THREE AND a half years I spent in Lee University's Campus Choir changed my whole life. We traveled the world singing in hundreds of churches and conferences. I learned so much about ministry that has forever shaped me into the pastor I am today. Dr. David Horton was the director at that time but has since breathed his last breath here on earth and is enjoying the prize that is promised to those who follow Jesus. Although he is no longer with us, Dr. Horton (or "Doc," as we would call him) is one of the first who comes to mind when I talk about my mentors. He left a legacy that I am still learning from to this day.

> ## THERE SHOULDN'T BE AN "ON" AND "OFF" SWITCH IN THE WAY WE LIVE OUR LIVES.

In 2003, Campus Choir was invited to lead worship in Nashville, Tennessee, at the Trinity Broadcasting Network (TBN)
studio. It was my senior year of college, and I was taking every
opportunity to cherish the time I had left with the choir that had
already so strongly impacted my life. We were all super excited,
honored, and pretty nervous because this would not be recorded;
it would be a "live" service broadcast all over the world. I loved
moments like that in the choir because Doc always made sure we
treated the people at every place that invited us with honor. He
always wanted us to be genuine, passionate, and honoring in our
worship rather than compromise our influence from ignorance
about how to act before or after the services. There shouldn't be
an "on" and "off" switch in the way we live our lives. That's not
integrity, and that's definitely not trustworthy. I was taught to be
the same on and off the stage. That's integrity!

So, off to Nashville we went, led by our fearless leader. I always
thought Doc was brave (or crazy) to lead about one hundred college students all over the world in his sixties. We left our classes
early that day so that we could have plenty of time to make the
drive from Cleveland to Nashville, get set up, and have the proper
sound checks before service started. We knew it would be a long
day and night because the service was in the evening, and we
would be driving back following the service. We arrived at the
studio as scheduled and kicked things into high gear so that we
were ready and prepared.

As service started, I remember thinking, *Man, these lights are
really hot.* This was before LED lights, when only big par can
lights were available. Those things could put off the heat! Those

lights, combined with the suits we had to wear, made for a really sweaty experience. In that studio, the choir stood on risers, and we always had to line up and pack in pretty tight to accommodate everyone. So, if the person next to me got excited during worship and started jumping, then I was probably jumping with them, and vice versa. Campus Choir is not a performance choir but a Spirit-filled worshiping choir, so service length was unpredictable. That night was no different. Doc led us with so much passion as we worshiped God for over an hour! It was amazing!

Perry Stone was scheduled to preach that night, and we stayed right there with him on stage during his whole sermon. This is no knock on Perry Stone, but because of his intelligence and the detail in which he breaks down the Word of God, he preaches for a while sometimes. That's not a bad thing. It just is what it is because of how thoroughly he unpacks the Scriptures.

> **NEVER ASK SOMEONE TO DO SOMETHING THAT YOU'RE NOT WILLING TO DO YOURSELF.**

We had traveled for several hours, set up for a couple of hours, sang our guts out for over an hour, and then continued to stand on those risers for another hour. After he preached, there was an altar call, and we sang more songs while people responded and received prayer. It was an incredible night! Was it hot? Yes. Was I sweating?

Tons! Were my legs getting tired? Absolutely! Was it getting late? Yes. At one point during the sermon, I remember looking down at Dr. Horton just to make sure he was okay. He didn't sit down with the congregation on the front row; he stood at the end of the risers with us during the whole service. I remember leaning over to the guy beside me and saying, "I feel bad for Doc. I wish he'd go sit down."

When service was over, and we were breaking everything down, I walked over to Doc to check on him. I put my hand on his back and asked, "Doc, are you okay? I felt so bad that you had to stand there with us the whole time. I was hoping you would go sit down." In response, Doc wrapped his arm around my shoulder and walked me to the side of the room. For a second, I thought I had upset or offended him. When we reached the side of the room, he said in his awesome, low voice, "Uh, Brother Justin, in ministry and in leadership, you will learn never to ask anyone to do something that you're not willing to do yourself." I replied, "Yes, sir." Then he walked off, leaving me speechless—my mind had been rocked! So many moments changed my life in Campus Choir, but that moment marked me. Never ask someone to do something that you're not willing to do yourself. That was one of the many reasons why I trusted Doc. That's also one of the many reasons why God trusted Moses. I pray that this will be one of the reasons why God and others will trust you!

THERE'S A LEADER IN YOU

John Maxwell said, "Everything rises and falls on leadership" in his book *Developing the Leader Within You.*[26] If you want to be a

---

26 John C. Maxwell, *Developing the Leader Within You* (Nashville, TN: Thomas Nelson, 2005).

great leader, you will have to become disciplined and work hard to get there. You will also find that a great leader is trustworthy. The Lord said in Numbers 12:7 (NLT, author addition), "Of all my house, [Moses] is the one I trust." The Bible never directly states that Moses was a great leader. The Bible says that Moses was trustworthy. So, because Moses was trustworthy, he was a great leader. I'm challenging you to become a leader who others can trust. You might be thinking, *I'm not called to be a leader.* You're wrong! Everyone is leading someone. If you're a parent, you're leading your kids. If you're a coach, you're leading your players. If you're a doctor or nurse, you're leading your patients. If you're a teacher, you're leading your students. If you have a job, you're leading your co-workers. If you're a manager, you're leading your staff. If you're a student, you're leading your peers. If you're a pastor, you're leading your church. *Everyone is leading someone, so don't be the reason why others develop trust issues.* Be a leader others can trust!

LEAD BY EXAMPLE

Remember the Titans is based on a true story and is arguably one of the greatest movies of all time. The movie has so many valuable leadership and life lessons and is a great illustration of not expecting others to do something that you aren't willing to do yourself. It was set during a volatile time in America when Black schools and White schools were merging together as one. Sadly, not everyone was for that, which created some hostile racial environments. The football team at T. C. Williams High School had to deal with that racial conflict head-on. Gerry

Bertier was the captain of the White team, and Julius Campbell was the captain of the Black team. They were tasked with somehow bringing unity to both sides to become one team. In one heated argument during their first few days of practice, Bertier called Campbell out for his lack of effort and for not obeying his leadership, and Campbell returned this accusation with an honest reply—Bertier's White teammates refused to block for Campbell's Black teammates. Campbell's attitude frustrated Bertier. It was Bertier's job to call his White teammates to a higher standard, but instead, he blindly trusted them to do the right thing. Bertier had no accountability to ensure his White teammates cooperated, so Campbell became frustrated with Bertier's hypocrisy. In response, Campbell said, "Attitude reflects leadership!" In other words, Bertier had a bad attitude and wasn't leading by example. Campbell couldn't trust him because of his hypocrisy—he was causing trust issues! So, Bertier took that to heart and started to hold his White teammates accountable. As a result, Bertier eliminated Campbell's trust issues because he decided to lead by example.

Be a trustworthy leader by giving people a good example to follow! News flash: You can't expect others to do something that you're not willing to do. Don't expect your staff to clean toilets if you're not willing to do it. Don't expect your friends not to gossip when you're doing it yourself. Don't expect your spouse to treat you with respect when you're not willing to do it yourself. That's hypocritical leadership, and that's not trustworthy!

It seems like the Israelites didn't trust Moses because of all the times that they grumbled, complained, and turned their backs on him, but really, they were just losing their minds, and unfortunately, that's one of the ugly parts of leadership. Through it all, Moses was never hypocritical, and he continued to lead by example. No one can lead millions of people out of slavery and into freedom without being a trustworthy leader! God gave Moses His blessings and favor because Moses earned His trust. I believe that God is always looking for people He can trust so that He can use them to lead others. I pray that you will respond to the challenge and start living a life that others can trust and follow. If you lead with integrity and by example, then God's favor will always be on your life.

W.W.J.D.

When someone mentions *The Last Supper*, our minds visualize Leonardo da Vinci's famous painting with twelve pale white men sitting in a straight line with Jesus in the middle. Buckle up because that image doesn't accurately represent that scene!

I'll never forget the first time I spent the night at Jeronne Hale's house, one of my best friends from high school. We had just finished eating dinner, and with a smirk on his face, he said, "Graham, I want to show you something." He turned the hallway lights on, led me to a picture on their wall, and just waited for me to respond. I looked up and saw the first ever Black person *Last Supper*! (Spoiler alert: Jeronne is Black, and I'm White.) We both just stood there staring quietly for what felt like twenty seconds. Suddenly, both of us just started laughing hysterically at the same time because we were embracing the fact that neither one of us actually had it right.

It was one of those brotherly laughs where you hit the other person, fall into things, and then cry from laughing so hard. This solidified the fact that Jeronne and I were more than just friends—we were real brothers!

> **TRUSTWORTHY LEADERS ARE NEVER TOO PRIDEFUL TO HUMBLE THEMSELVES BEFORE THE ONES THEY LEAD.**

The Bible explains in all four Gospels (Matthew, Mark, Luke, and John) that Jesus knew it was time for Him to do what He had been sent to do—to be crucified on the cross for the sins of the world. It was during the time of the Passover Festival, so Jesus had the disciples prepare a supper together. You must understand that everything Jesus did was intentional. This was the last time they would all gather with Him before His death, so He wanted to teach the disciples the world's greatest leadership principles.

TRUSTWORTHY LEADERS ARE ALWAYS . . . HUMBLE

At this gathering, Jesus washed the disciples' feet, which is one of the best examples of humility. Back then, washing someone's feet was far more unpleasant than it would be today. We have showers, socks, and shoes. They walked on dirt roads and floors with only sandals. So, their feet would have been extremely dirty. This was a lesson in humility. If the King of kings and the Savior of the world would humble Himself to such a lowly position, then we need to take note of that. Trustworthy leaders are never too prideful to humble themselves before the ones they lead. Jesus was showing them that if they were going to change the world, then they would have to do it with humility. James 4:10 (NIV, author addition) teaches us to "Humble [ourselves] before the Lord, and he will lift [us] up. Philippians 2:3 (NLT) says, "Be humble, thinking of others as better than yourselves." Scripture goes on to say in verse 9 that because Jesus humbled Himself in obedience, "God exalted him to the highest place and gave him the name that is above every name" (NIV). *Humility is simply recognizing that your position as a trustworthy leader is to help others discover their God-given purpose.* Humility is not selfish. Humility is caring for the needs of others. Humility isn't interested in making a name for itself. Humility is working hard to assist others and celebrating when they succeed in life. If you are a humble leader, you will gain the trust of others.

WHEN YOU TRUST OTHERS, THEY WILL TRUST YOU.

Moses was also an example of humility. In fact, Numbers 12:3 (NIV) says that "Moses was a very humble man, more humble than anyone else on the face of the earth."When Moses started the journey with the Israelites after the miracle of the Red Sea and defeating Pharaoh, he did his best to meet the needs of the people. His plan was to meet with each person to help them through any problem that arose. He met with people from sunup to sundown to prove himself a trustworthy leader. When Moses's father-in-law visited them, he showed Moses a better leadership model that would benefit the entire nation—to raise up leaders who could help him with those meetings. This delegation approach would encourage others to get involved, be much more efficient, and keep him from losing his mind. Moses wasn't too prideful to take advice from someone else. It takes a humble person to admit that someone else has a better idea than you. For the record, I follow the leadership model that Moses's father-in-law put in place. Am I *willing* to meet with anyone and everyone? Yes. Is it *possible*? No. So, I have worked hard to empower leaders and staff to help me carry that load. It's extremely prideful to think that you're the only one who can help people. In fact, humility is believing in other people's gifts and trusting them to help you lead. When you trust others, they will trust you. Humility eliminates trust issues!

TRUSTWORTHY LEADERS ARE . . . COMPASSIONATE

To understand the next two principles, we have to understand Jewish culture, traditions, and customs. During that time, no one ate at a standard table like we see in paintings. Instead, tables were U-shaped and placed in the middle with couches along the three sides, called the triclinium. Another important detail is that everyone was seated in a specific spot, and every spot had a designated title. The host of the meal would sit two spots from the left. The host of this meal, the Last Supper, was Jesus. The guest of honor would sit on his left. According to Matthew 26:23, that person was Judas. That's crazy because Judas was the one who would betray Jesus. Jesus was teaching us to show the greatest of love to the worst of sinners! Trustworthy leaders are compassionate.

The guest of honor was special to the host. Judas was with Jesus through everything! The miracles. The signs. The wonders. The teachings. He was so close to Jesus, but at the same time, his heart was so far from God. I know that there had to be a Judas for God's plan to come to fruition, but we can't skip past the heart of compassion that Jesus had for him. Some would say that Judas was the worst of sinners because he was close to Jesus but still stabbed Him in the back. That may be true, but it still didn't stop Jesus from giving him a seat at the table.

> **COMPASSION WILL ENABLE OTHERS TO TRUST YOU BECAUSE THEY WILL SEE THE LOVE OF GOD IN YOU!**

You might think that you're the worst of sinners, but *you can trust Jesus because He is so compassionate!* No matter what you've done and no matter where you've been, Jesus has made a place for you in hopes that you'll come and sit with Him at the table!

So, for every sinner . . . there's a place for you!

For every alcoholic . . . there's a place for you!

For every two-faced, back-stabbing liar . . . there's a place for you!

For every hypocrite . . . there's a place for you!

For every arrogant, religious person . . . there's a place for you!

For every busted-up, jacked-up, and messed-up person . . . there's a place for you!

Jesus has made a seat for you at the table. It's your choice to join in, and it's your choice to walk away!

If you want to be a leader that people trust, then be compassionate towards others! Don't be so quick to write people off when they mess up. Always remember that you're far from perfect too. Moses was also a compassionate leader. God's declaration that Moses was the one He trusted came on the heels of Aaron and Miriam dishonoring and disrespecting God and Moses. The Lord became very angry with Aaron and Miriam and even struck Miriam with leprosy. Instead of responding with self-righteousness and bitterness, Moses was compassionate and pleaded with God to heal Miriam. Because of his compassion, Moses gained even more credibility with Aaron and Miriam. Compassion does not hold on to unforgiveness. Compassion is loving and exercises grace. Compassion will enable others to trust you because they will see the love of God in you! Compassion eliminates trust issues!

TRUSTWORTHY LEADERS . . . SERVE

Everything Jesus did was on purpose. So, when we pick apart the seating arrangements at the Last Supper, we get a glimpse of what I would call the highest level of leadership. Leading up to this meal, the disciples constantly argued. In Matthew 18:1 (NIV), the disciples wanted to know "who . . . is the greatest in the kingdom of heaven?" In Mark 9:34 (NIV), the disciples "argued about who was the greatest." Jesus then tried to explain to them in verse 35 (NIV) that "anyone who wants to be first must be the very last, and servant of all." In Luke 22:24 (NIV), when the Last Supper finally took place, they were still arguing "as to which of them was considered the greatest." At one point, it got so bad that even James and John's mother got involved! In Matthew 20:20-24, she ran to Jesus and asked Him to make her sons His favorites. When the other ten found out, they were ticked at James and John. It was like a good old-fashioned "Yo Momma!" battle! Jesus shut them up in Matthew 20:26-28 (NLT) when He said,

> *"Whoever wants to be a leader among you must be your servant, and whoever wants to be first among you must become your slave. For even the Son of Man came not to be served but to serve others and to give his life as a ransom for many."*

In other words, trustworthy leaders will learn how to serve!

Remember, Jesus hosted this meal, and Judas was in the seat of the guest of honor. The person who sat on the host's right side would be the trusted friend. We can gather that John was that trusted friend, according to John 13:23. This is where things get interesting.

GREAT LEADERS WILL EARN TRUST BY LEARNING TO SERVE OTHERS.

In many people's eyes, the servant's seat, which sat at the end on the opposite side of the host, was the least important. The person in that seat would serve the others during the meal and ensure that everyone had what they needed, as well as wash everyone's feet. We see in John 13:24 that Peter was assigned to that seat because of how he motioned to John to ask him a question. We also know it was Peter's seat because he was convicted when Jesus started washing their feet. Peter knew that was supposed to be his job. Peter was the chief apostle. He was the leader of the pack. He was the hot head. He was the big mouth. He was the radical one. He was the one who walked on water. Peter! Jesus was showing us that great leaders will earn trust by learning to serve others. Peter's placement at the table was not dishonorable by any means. It was definitely not inferior to the other disciples. It was actually preparation for what Jesus would trust Peter to do down the road. Spoiler alert for those who haven't read the book of Acts in the Bible: It was roughly fifty days after this dinner that Peter would preach his first sermon and witness three thousand people give their lives to Christ—in one service! *God trusts servant leaders to change the world!*

Most families have an unspoken understanding of who sits where at the dinner table. In the Graham house, I sit at the end near the wall beside my wife, and Jocy and Judah sit on the other side of her. One night, my son, Judah, started to sit down at the opposite end of the table across from me but then quickly changed his mind. He said, "Ya know, I'm not going to sit here at the butt of the table." We all busted out laughing while he said, "Dad, you're sitting at the head of the table, and that would make this the butt, and I'm not the butt of the family!" We had never mentioned anything about the "head of the table," but my son had figured it out. I took that moment to say, "Judah, it's really all in your perspective. You'll never be able to sit in my chair until you embrace and learn how to enjoy sitting in that chair." He then accused me of calling him the "butt," and we laughed some more.

> **TRUSTWORTHY LEADERS DON'T PICK UP TITLES. THEY PICK UP TOWELS AND SERVE!**

You'll never know how to be great until you learn how to serve. Trustworthy leaders make reservations at the table to serve. If you want to earn trust, then sit in the servant's seat! Jesus placed Peter in that seat to teach him humility and servanthood. He washed their feet to show them that no one is too good to serve, and anyone who serves can be great. Martin Luther King, Jr. said,

"Everyone can be great because everybody can serve."[27] If you want to be trusted, then learn how to serve others. If you want God to trust you, then learn how to humble yourself and serve. If you ever want to rise to great heights, then learn how to serve in low places. *The highest level of leadership is to serve others!* Lawrence D. Bell said, "Show me a man who cannot be bothered to do little things, and I'll show you a man who cannot be trusted to do big things."[28] If you want to eliminate trust issues with God and other people, then learn to faithfully serve in the little things! Run a few errands for your spouse. Pick up a coffee for your co-worker. Get involved at a church and volunteer on Sundays and/or throughout the week. Find a need in someone else's life and meet that need. The key to greatness is serving others. Trustworthy leaders don't pick up titles. They pick up towels and serve! Serving others eliminates trust issues!

SAY, "YES!"

Trustworthy leaders say "yes" to God when He calls them to lead. Moses was faithful in the little things on the backside of the desert when God called him to serve His people. Was he perfect? No. Was he qualified? No. Did he agree to obey and follow God? Yes. God took Moses's "yes" and changed the world. Moses earned God's trust with his "yes." Moses earned other people's trust with his "yes." Of all God's people, will you be one He can trust? If you want to earn God's trust, then say "yes." If you want others to trust you, then say "yes."

---

27 King, Martin, Jr. "The Drum Major Instinct." Sermon, Ebenezer Baptist Church, April 4, 1968, 29:51, https://www.youtube.com/watch?v=Mefbog-b4-4.
28 Lawrence D. Bell, "Show me a man . . . to do big things," *Bell Aircraft Museum*, https://bellaircraftmuseum.org/.

Say "yes" to surrender!
Say "yes" to faithfulness!
Say "yes" to integrity!
Say "yes" to discipline!
Say "yes" to repentance!
Say "yes" to redemption!
Say "yes" to humility!
Say "yes" to compassion!
Say "yes" to serving!
Say "yes" to following God!
Say "yes" to Jesus!

This world needs people they can trust. Do whatever it takes to earn it. Your spouse needs you! Your family needs you! Your team needs you! Your friends need you! Your church needs you! Your work needs you! Don't miss this: You need people that you can trust too! So, don't expect someone to do something that you're unwilling to do yourself. Trust starts with you! I believe in you, and God has a big plan for you! Work to eliminate your trust issues today so God can use you to change the world for His glory! *God is looking for trustworthy people.*

Will He find that in you?

HERE'S THE BIG IDEA:

Say "YES!" to God if you want to eliminate trust issues. Your "yes" will come with discipline, hard work, and leading by example but will be totally worth it. Anything of great value will come at a high cost. Gaining trust is worth it!

CONSIDER:

- Do you feel like you have hypocritical tendencies?
- Do you expect things from others that you don't even do yourself?
- Have you had good leadership examples in your life?
- Have they modeled integrity and trustworthiness?
- How well do you lead with humility, compassion, and servanthood?
- Is there anything or anyone holding you back from saying "yes" to the discipline needed to eliminate trust issues in your life?

CHALLENGE:

- Reach out to the people in your life who have set a trustworthy example for you to follow, and spend time expressing your gratitude for them. Get specific with them regarding some moments that impacted you the most.
- Find a mentor or an accountability partner who will continue to challenge you in the area of trust.
- Be intentional every day to humble yourself before God in prayer, worship, and the Word. Make some goals and list the action steps necessary to help you become a trustworthy person.

PRAYER:

Heavenly Father,

Thank You for being the One I can always trust! Thank You for Your Son, Jesus, who set the greatest example for me to live by. Please forgive me for the times that I have come up short of that standard. Will you give me the mind of Christ so that I can take the necessary steps to eliminate any trust issues in my life? I recognize that my actions speak louder than my words. Make me sensitive to the voice of the Holy Spirit so that I can avoid making hypocritical decisions that would break trust with You and others. Give me clean hands and a pure heart. Now, may the words of my mouth and the meditations of my heart be acceptable in Your sight, oh Lord, my Strength, and my Redeemer. In Jesus's name. Amen!

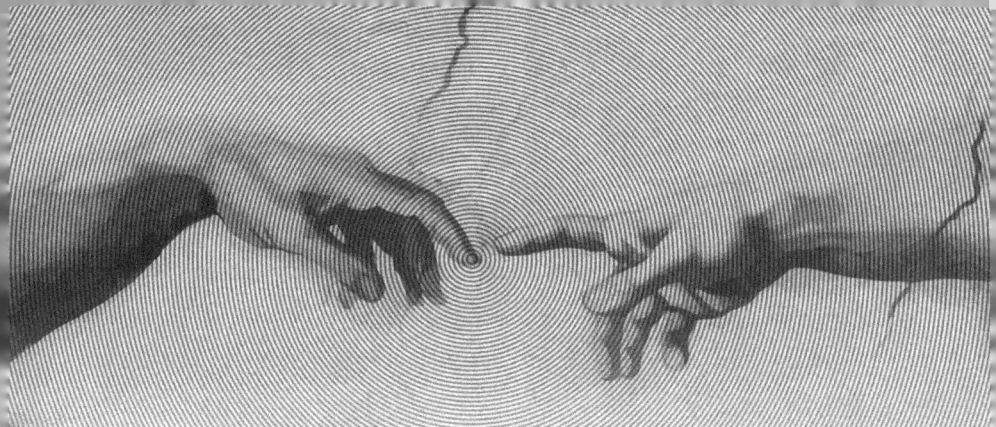

PAY THE PRICE

ANYTHING OF GREAT value will come at a high cost. Eliminating the trust issues in your life will cost you. It will be challenging. It will seem exhausting. It will cause you frustration. It will require your honesty and humility. But . . . it will all be worth it! I want to be a trustworthy person for God. I want to be a trustworthy person for my wife and my kids, Jocy and Judah. I don't want to be the reason for their trust issues. Our journey starts now, and it will never stop. Giving and gaining trust must be continually and intentionally cultivated to maintain integrity. My prayer is that you will do whatever it takes for God to look at you and say . . .

"Of all my house, _____ is the one I trust."

I challenge you to work hard so that, one day, you can confidently fill that space with your name. You might be thinking, *I don't know if I can do that or if I'll ever be able to do that.* I believe you can because you're going to do whatever it takes to eliminate trust issues! If you don't know where to start, consider starting here.

If you don't have a relationship with God or have drifted away from God, allow me to lead you in a prayer that will forever change your life. Pray this prayer from your heart and your mouth:

God,

Thank You for loving me. Thank You for never giving up on me. I need Your grace and mercy. I believe in You. I believe in Your Son, Jesus. I believe that He died for my sins and rose from the dead. Jesus, I confess that You are Lord! Please forgive me of my sins. From this day forward, I will not run from You. I will run to You because You love me, and You are my Savior! Give me strength, wisdom, and grace each and every day to make decisions that are pleasing to You. Thank You for helping me put my trust in You. Will You help me live in a way that builds Your trust in me? In Jesus's name. Amen!"

If you prayed that prayer for the first time or maybe recommitted your life to Jesus, I would love to hear from you! Scan the QR code at the bottom of the page, and let's connect!

I strongly encourage you to get connected to a church near you that believes that Jesus is the only way to heaven. You can also join us at The Avenue Church or on our online campus. Check us out at www.theavenuemorristown.com and on all social media platforms and YouTube. I hope to see you soon! Until then . . . let's pay the price, start climbing, and eliminate TRUST ISSUES!

AVAIL
PODCAST

LISTEN WHEREVER YOU GET YOUR PODCASTS
AVAIL LEADERSHIP PODCAST

FOLLOW THE LEADER

STAY CONNECTED

facebook.com/TheArtofAvail   @theartofavail   AVAIL

www.ingramcontent.com/pod-product-compliance
Lightning Source LLC
Chambersburg PA
CBHW070538090426
42735CB00013B/3017